Death and Dying

A Bibliography (1950-1974)

Death and Dying
A Bibliography (1950-1974)

by

G. Howard Poteet

The Whitston Publishing Company

Troy, New York

1976

PREFACE

This bibliography documents literature on death
and dying. The listings generally have little to do
with euthanasia, nothing to do with legal interpretations of death and life, and do not include suicide.
Instead, the central point of the work is almost exclusively the psychology of death. In this rather
specific area, this volume attempts to be a near com-
plete world bibliography for the years 1950 through
1974.

The subject headings have emerged from the mater-
ial instead of being imposed on the matter by external
lists. In addition, adequate "See' and "See Also"
entries are included.

The following bibliographies and serials indexes,
among others, have been searched in compiling this work:
APPLIED SCIENCE AND TECHNOLOGY INDEX; BIBLIOGRAPHIC IN-
DEX; BIOLOGICAL AND AGRICULTURAL INDEX; BOOK REVIEW
DIGEST; BOOKS IN PRINT; BOOKS: SUBJECTS; CUMULATIVE
BOOK INDEX; CURRENT INDEX TO JOURNALS IN EDUCATION;
EDUCATION INDEX; HOSPITAL LITERATURE INDEX; INDEX MED-
ICUS; LIBRARY OF CONGRESS CATALOG; LONDON BIBLIOGRAPHY
OF THE SOCIAL SCIENCES; THE NEW YORK TIMES INDEX; PUB-
LIC AFFAIRS INFORMATION SERVICE; READERS GUIDE TO PERI-
ODICAL LITERATURE; SOCIAL SCIENCES AND HUMANITIES INDEX;
SOCIOLOGICAL ABSTRACTS.

This bibliography is designed for use by researchers at all levels in sociology, medicine, education,
and allied areas. Comments, corrections, and sugges-
tions will be appreciated.

G. Howard Poteet
New York City

LIST OF ABBREVIATIONS

ABBREVIATIONS	TITLE
AARN New Lett	Alberta Association of Registered Nurses (Edmonton, Alberta, Canada)
AORN J	AORN Journal (Englewood, California)
Acta Med Scand	Acta Medica Scandinavia (Stockholm)
Acta Neuroveg	Acta Neurovegetativa (Wien)
Acta Paediatr Acad Sci Hung	Acta Paediatrica Academe Scientarium Hungaricae (Budapest)
Acta Paedopsychiatr	Acta Paedopsychiatrica (Basel)
Acta Psychiat Scand	Acta Psychiatricia Scandinavia (Copenhaven)
Adolescence	Adolescence (Roslyn Heights, New York)
Adult Lead	Adult Leadership (Washington)
Agnes Karll Schwest	Die Agnes Karll-Schwester (Frankfurt)
Ala J Med Sci	Alabama Journal of Medical Sciences (Birmingham)
Alum Mag	Alumni Magazine (Johns Hopkins) (Baltimore)
America	America (New York)
Am Anthrop	American Anthropologist (Washington)
Am Behav Sci	American Behavioral Scientist (New York)
Am Coll Health Ass	Journal of the American College Health Association (Ithaca)
Am Geriat Soc	American Geriatrics Society Journal (New York)
Am Heart J	American Heart Journal (St. Louis)
Am Imago	American Imago (New York)
Am J Clin Hypn	American Journal of Clinical Hypnosis (Minneapolis)
Am J Dis Child	American Journal of Diseases of Children (Chicago)

Am J Nurs or AJN	American Journal of Nursing (New York)
Am J Occup Therap	American Journal of Occupational Therapy (New York)
Am J Orthopsychiat	American Journal of Orthopsychiatry (New York)
Am J Psychiat	American Journal of Psychiatry (Hanover, New Hampshire)
Am J Psychotherap	American Journal of Psychotherapy (Lancaster)
Am J Pub Health	American Journal of Public Health and the Nation's Health (New York)
Am Nurs Ass Conv Clin Sess	American Nurses Association Convention Clinical Sessions (New York)
Amer Pract Dig Treat	American Practitioner and Digest of Treatment (New York)
Am Psych Ass J	American Psychoanalysis Association Journal (New York)
Am Soc Rev	American Sociological Review (New York)
Ana Clin Sess	American Nurses Association Clinical Sessions (New York)
Ana Res Clin Conf	American Nurses Association Research Clinical Conference (New York)
Ann Intern Med	Annals of Internal Medicine (Philadelphia)
Ann Medicopsychol	Annales Medico-Psychologiques (Paris)
Ann N Y Acad Sci	Annals of the New York Academy of Sciences (New York)
Annals Amer Acad Pol Soc Sci	Annals of the American Academy of Political Social Science (New York)
Arch Franc Pediat	Archives Francaises de Pediatrie (Paris)
Arch Gen Psychiat	Archives of General Psychiatry (Chicago)
Arch Neur and Path	Archives of Neurology and Psychiatry (New York)

Ass Clin Lab Sci	Annals of Clinical Laboratory Science (Philadelphia)
Atlan	Atlantic Monthly (Boston)
Atlas	Atlas (Paris)
Aust Nurses J	Australian Nurses Journal (Sydney, Australia)
Az Med	Arizona Medicine (Scottsdale, Arizona)
Bedside Nurse	Bedside Nurse (New York)
Behav Sci	Behavioral Science (Ann Arbor)
Bet Home & Gard	Better Homes and Gardens (Des Moines)
Black Bag	Black Bag (Bristol, England)
Brill	Brill (New York)
Brit J Med Psychol	British Journal of Medical Psychology (London)
Brit J Prev Med Soc	British Journal of Preventive and Social Medicine (London)
Brit J Psychiat	British Journal of Psychiatry (London)
Brit Med J	British Medical Journal (London)
Bull Am Coll Surg	Bulletin of the American College of Surgeons (Chicago)
Bull Am Prot Hosp Ass	Bulletin of the American Protestant Hospital Association (Chicago)
Bull Infirm Cath Can	Bulletin des Infirmieres Catholiques de Canada (Quebec)
Bull L A Co Med Ass	Bulletin of the Los Angeles County Medical Association (Los Angeles)
Bull Menninger Clin	Bulletin of the Menninger Clinic (Topeka)
Bull N Y Acad Med	Bulletin of the New York Academy of Medicine (New York)
CA	CA: Cancer Journal for Clinicians (New York)
CA: Bull Cancer Prog	CA: Bulletin of Cancer Progress (New York)
CCAR Yrbk	Central Conference of American Rabbis Yearbook (Cincinnati)

Cah Anesth	Cahiers D'Anesthesiologie (Paris)
Can Ment Health	Canada's Mental Health (Ottawa)
Can Anesth	Canadian Anaesthetist's Society Journal (Toronto)
Can Doctor	Canadian Doctor (Quebec)
Can Hosp	Canadian Hospital (Toronto)
Can J Pub Health	Canadian Journal of Public Health (Toronto)
Can Med Ass J	Canadian Medical Association Journal (Toronto)
Can Psychiat Ass J	Canadian Psychiatric Association Journal (Ottawa)
Cancer	Cancer (Philadelphia)
Cath Nurse	Catholic Nurse (Washington)
Cath World	Catholic World (New York)
Cesk Gynekol	Ceskoslovenska Gynekologie (Prague)
Chicago Med Schl Q	Chicago Medical School Quarterly (Chicago)
Child	Children (Washington)
Child Dev	Child Development (Lafayette, Indiana)
Child Ed	Childhood Education (Washington)
Child Study	Child Study (New York)
Chr Cent	Christian Century (Chicago)
Christ Med Soc J	Christian Medical Society Journal (Chicago)
Christ Nurs	Christian Nurse (Nagpur, India)
Clergy Rev	Clergy Review (New York)
Cleve Clin Q	Cleveland Clinic Quarterly (Cleveland)
Clin Pediat	Clinical Pediatrics (Philadelphia)
Clin Proc Child Hosp	Clinical Proceedings of the Children's Hospital (Washington)
Coll Gen Pract	College of General Practitioners (Royal) (London)
Commentary	Commentary (New York)
Commonweal	Commonweal (New York)
Commun Ment Health	Community Mental Health Journal (New York)
Commun Psychiat	Community Hospital and Psychiatry (Washington)

Compr Nurs Q	Comprehensive Nurses Quarterly (Tokyo)
Compr Psychia	Comprehensive Psychiatry (New York)
Concours Med	Concours Medical (Paris)
Confin Psychiat	Confina Psychiatrica (Basel)
Conn Med	Connecticut Medicine (New Haven)
Cons Jud	Conservative Judaism (New York)
Consult	Consultant (Philadelphia)
Contemp Surgery	Contemporary Surgery (New York)
Coronet	Coronet (New York)
Crit Care Med	Critical Care Medicine (New York)
Curr Med News	Current Medical News (New York)
Curr Psychiat Therap	Current Psychiatric Therapies (New York)
Del Med J	Delaware Medical Journal (Wilmington)
Deutsch Med Wschr	Deutsche Medizinische Wochen-schrift (Stuttgart)
Deutsch Z Ges Gerichtl Med	Deutsche Zeitschrift Fuer Gesamte Gerichtliche Med-izin (Stuttgart)
Dev Med Child Neurol	Developmental Medicine and Child Neurology (London)
Dev Psych	Developmental Psychobiology (New York)
Dis Ment Syst	Diseases of the Mental System (New York)
Dis Nerv Syst	Diseases of the Nervous Sys-tem (Galveston)
Dist Nurs	District Nursing (London)
Duodecim	Duodecim (Helsinki)
Dtsch Krankenpflegez	Deutsche Krankenpflegezeit-schrift- Deutsche Schwest-ernzeitung (Stuttgart)
Ebony	Ebony (Chicago)
Educ	Education (Appleton, Wisconsin)
Ed Lead	Educational Leadership (Washington)
Ed Theory	Educational Theory (Urbana, Illinois)

El Schl J	Elementary School Journal (Chicago)
Emerg Med	Emergency Medicine (New York)
Encounter	Encounter (Indianapolis)
Eng J	English Journal (Urbana, Illinois)
Epheta	Epheta (Bogota)
Esquire	Esquire (New York)
Excep Child	Exceptional Children (Washington)
Excerpta Med	Excerpta Medica (Amsterdam)
Fam Coord	**Family Coordinator (Minneapolis)**
Fam Life Coord	Family Life Coordinator (Minneapolis)
Family Circle	Family Circle (New York)
Family Health	Family Health Bulletin (Berkeley)
Forest Hosp Pub	Forest Hospital Publications (Des Plaines, Illinois)
Frontiers of Hosp Psychiat (Roche Rept)	Frontiers of Hospital Psychiatry (Roche Report) (Nutley, New Jersey)
GAC Med Mex	Gaceta Medica de Mexico (Mexico)
Gen Psychol	Genetic Psychology Monographs (Provincetown)
Geog	Geography Journal (New York)
Geriatric Nurs	Geriatric Nursing (Minneapolis)
Geriatrics	Geriatrics (Minneapolis)
Geront	Gerontologist (Washington)
Geront Clin	Gerontologia Clinica (Basel)
GP	GP (Kansas City, Missouri)
Group Advance Psychiat	Group for the Advancement of Psychiatry: Symposium (New York)
Guys Hosp Reports	Guy's Hospital Reports (London)
Harefuah	Harefuah (Tel Aviv)
Harper	Harper's Monthly Magazine (New York)
Harvard Med Alum Bull	Harvard Medical Alumni Bulletin (Cambridge)
Harvard Theol	Harvard Theology (Cambridge)
Hawaii	Hawaii Medical Journal (Honolulu)

Heal Hum Behavior	Journal of Health and Human Behavior (Washington)
Health Servs Reps	Health Service Reports (Rockville, Maryland)
Health Soc Serv J	Health and Social Service Journal (London)
Heart and Lung	Heart and Lung (St. Louis)
Heb Med J	Hebrew Medical Journal (New York)
Hippokrates	Hippokrates (Stuttgart)
Hobbies	Hobbies (Chicago)
Hosp	Hospitals (Chicago)
Hosp Commun Psychiat	Hospital and Community Psychiatry (Washington)
Hosp Mgmt	Hospital Management (Chicago)
Hosp Phys	Hospital Physician (Oradell, New Jersey)
Hosp Pract	Hospital Practice (New York)
Hosp Progress	Hospital Progress (St. Louis)
Hosp Top	Hospital Topics (New York)
Hosp Tribune	Hospital Tribune (New York)
Hosp World	Hospital World (London)
Hudson	Hudson Review (New York)
Human Relations	Human Relations (New York)
Humanitas	Humanitas (Pittsburgh)
Ill Lon News	Illustrated London News (London)
Ill Med J	Illinois Medical Journal (Chicago)
Imprint	Imprint (New York)
In J Ped	Indian Journal of Pediatrics (Calcutta)
Ind J Soc Res	Indian Journal of Social Research (Meerut, India)
Ind St Med Ass	Indiana State Medical Association (Indiana)
Infirm Can	Infirmiere Canadienne (Montreal)
Instr	Instructor (Dannsville, New York)
Int J Addict	International Journal of the Addictions (New York)
Int J Group Psycho- therap	International Journal of Group Psychotherapy (New York)
Int J Neuropsychiat	International Journal of Neuropsychiatry (Chicago)

Int J Nurs Studies	International Journal of Nursing Studies (Elmsford, New York)
Int J Psychiat	International Journal of Psychiatry (New York)
Int J Psychoanal	International Journal of Psychoanalysis (London)
Int J Relig Ed	International Journal of Religious Education (London)
Int J Soc Psychiat	International Journal of Social Psychiatry (London)
Int Nurs Rev	International Nursing Review (London)
Int Philos Q	International Philosophical Quarterly (Bronx, New York)
Int Surgery	International Surgery (Chicago)
Irish J Med Sci	Irish Journal of Medical Science (Dublin)
Irish Nurs News	Irish Nursing News (Dublin)
Isr Ann Psychiat	Israel Annals of Psychiatry and Related Disciplines (Jerusalem)
JAMA	Journal of the American Medical Association (Chicago)
J Abnorm Psychol	Journal of Abnormal Psychology (Washington)
J Abnorm Soc Psych	Journal of Abnormal and Social Psychology (Washington)
J Am Acad Child Psychiat	Journal of the American Academy of Child Psychiatry (New York)
J Am Coll Dent	Journal of the American College of Dentists (Fulton, New York)
J Am Coll Health Ass	Journal of the American College Health Association (Ithaca)
J Am Dent Assoc	Journal of the American Dental Association (Chicago)
J Am Med Wom Ass	Journal of the American Medical Women's Association (Nashville)
J Amer Geriat Soc	Journal of the American Geriatrics Society (Baltimore)
J Am Psychoanal Ass	Journal of the American Psychoanalytic Association (New York)

J Ind Med Ass	Journal of the Indiana State Medical Association (Indianapolis)
J Iowa Med Soc	Journal of the Iowa Medical Society (Des Moines, Iowa)
J Kansas Med Soc	Journal of the Kansas Medical Society (Topeka)
J Leg Med	Journal of Legal Medicine (New York)
J Louisiana Med Soc or J La Med Soc	Journal of the Louisiana Medical Society (New Orleans)
J Maine Med Ass	Journal of the Maine Medical Association (Brunswick, Maine)
J Med	Journal of Medicine (Basel)
J Med Ass Georgia	Journal of the Medical Association of Georgia (Atlanta)
J Med Ass Thai	Journal of the Medical Association of Thailand (Bangkok)
J Med Ed	Journal of Medical Education (Washington)
J Med Soc N J	Journal of the Medical Society of New Jersey (Trenton)
J Miss State Med Ass	Journal of the Mississippi State Medical Association (Jackson)
J Mount Sinai Hosp N Y	Journal of Mount Sinai Hospital, New York (New York)
J Nerv Ment Dis	Journal of Nervous and Mental Disease (Baltimore)
J Neurosurg Nurs	Journal of Neurosurgical Nursing (Chicago)
J Nurs	Journal of Nursing (Taipei)
J Nurs Ed	Journal of Nursing Education (New York)
J Pastor Care	Journal of Pastoral Care (New York)
J Pediat	Journal of Pediatrics (St. Louis)
J Person Soc Psych	Journal of Personality and Social Psychology (Washington)
J Personal	Journal of Personality (Durham, North Carolina)
J Philos	Journal of Philosophy (New York)
J Pract Nurs	Journal of Practical Nursing (New York)
J Psychiat Nurs	Journal of Psychiatric Nursing (Thorofare, New Jersey)

J Am Vet Med Ass	Journal of the American Veterinary Medical Association (Chicago)
J Autis Child Schizo	Journal of Autism and Childhood Schizophrenia (Washington)
J Child Psychol Psychiat	Journal of Child Psychology and Psychiatry and Allied Disciplines (London)
J Chron Dis	Journal of Chronic Diseases (St. Louis)
J Clin Psychol	Journal of Clinical Psychology (Brandon, Vermont)
J Coll Gen Pract	Journal of the College of General Practitioners (Royal) (Dartmouth, England)
J Commun Psychol	Journal of Community Psychology (Brandon, Vermont)
J Consult Clin Psychol	Journal of Clinical Psychology (Washington)
J Consult Psych	Journal of Consulting and Clinical Psychology (Washington)
J Contin Ed Nurs	Journal of Continuing Education in Nursing (Thorofare, New Jersey)
J Fla Med Ass	Journal of the Florida Medical Association (Jacksonville, Florida)
J Gen Psychol	Journal of General Psychology (Provincetown, Massachusetts)
J Gen Psychol or J Genet Psychol	Journal of Genetic Psychology (Provincetown, Massachusetts)
J Geront	Journal of Gerontology (St. Louis)
J Health Hum Behav	Journal of Health and Human Behavior (Washington)
J Health Soc Behav	Journal of Health and Social Behavior (Washington)
J Hill Hosp	Journal of Hillside Hospital (Glen Oaks, New York)
J Hist Med or J Med Hist	Journal of the History of Medicine and Allied Sciences (New Haven)
J Human Psych	Journal of Humanistic Psychology (San Francisco)
J Human Rel	Journal of Human Relations (Wilberforce, Ohio)

J Psychol	Journal of Psychology (Province-town)
J Psychosom Research	Journal of Psychosomatic Research (Elmsford, New York)
J R Coll Gen Pract	Journal of the Royal College of General Practitioners (Dartmouth, England)
J R Coll Phys Lond	Journal of the Royal College of Physicians of London (London)
J Rehab	Journal of Rehabilitation (Washington)
J Relig	Journal of Religion (Chicago)
J relig Ed	Journal of Religious Education (Nashville)
J Relig Health or J of Relig & Health	Journal of Religion and Health (Nashville)
J Sch Health	Journal of School Health (Columbus)
J Soc Issues	Journal of Social Issues (Ann Arbor, Michigan)
J Soc Psychol	Journal of Social Psychology (New York)
J Soc Serv Rev	Journal of Social Services Review (New York)
J Soc Work	Journal of Social Work (New York)
J Soc Work	Journal of Social Work and Education (New York)
J Tenn Med Ass	Journal of the Tennessee Medical Association (Nashville)
Jap J Nurs	Japan Journal of Nurse's Education (Tokyo)
Jap J Publ Health Nurs	Japan Journal of Public Health Nursing (Tokyo)
Journ of Health, Phys Ed, Rec or JOHPER	Journal of Health, Physical Education, Recreation (Washington)
Journ of Proj Tech & Personal Assess	Journal of Projective Techniques and Personality Assessment (Glendale, California)
Kango Kyoshitu	Kango Kyoshitu (Tokyo)
Kansas Nurs J	Kansas Nursing Journal (Topeka)
Ken Med Ass	Kentucky Medical Association Journal (Louisville)
Kenyon R	Kenyon Review (Nutley, New Jersey)
Klim Khir	Klinicheskaia Khirurgiia (Kiev)

Korean Nurs	Korean Nurse (Seoul)
Krankenpfl	Krankenpflege (Berlin)
Ladies Home J	Ladies Home Journal (New York)
Lakartidningen	Lakartidningen (Stockholm)
Lancet	Lancet (London)
Laval Med	Laval Medical (Quebec)
Life	Life (New York)
Lille Med	Lille Medical (Paris)
Maandschr Kindergen-eesk	Maanschr Kindergeneesk (Leiden)
Maryland Med J	Maryland State Medical Journal (Baltimore)
Matern Child Nurs J	Maternal Child Nursing Journal (Pittsburgh)
Mayo Clin Proc	Mayo Clinic Proceedings (Rochester, Minnesota)
McCalls	McCalls (New York)
Md Nurse	Maryland Nurse (Baltimore)
Med Ann D C	Medical Annals of the District of Columbia (Washington)
Med Clin N AM	Medical Clinics of North America (Philadelphia)
Med Ec	Medical Economics (New York)
Med Insight	Medical Insight (New York)
Med J Aust	Medical Journal of Australia (Sydney)
Med Klin	Medizinische Klinik (Munchen)
Med Leg Domm Copor	Medecine Legale et Dommace Corporel (Paris)
Med Sci Law	Medical Science and the Law (London)
Med Soc City N Y	Medical Society of the City of New York (New York)
Med Times	Medical Times (Manhasset)
Med Trib	Medical Tribune (New York)
Med Weit	Medizinische Weit (Stuttgart)
Med World News	Medical World News (New York)
Memphis Med J	Memphis and Mid-South Medical Journal (Memphis)
Ment Health	Mental Health (London)
Ment Hosp	Mental Hospital (Washington)
Mich Med	Michigan Medicine (East Lansing, Michigan)
Mich Nurs	Michigan Nurse (East Lansing, Michigan)
Midwest Q	Midwest Quarterly (Pittsburg, Kansas)
Midwife Health Visit	Midwife and Health Visitor (London)

Mind	Mind (Los Angeles)
Mind Psychiat Gen Pract	Mind Psychiatric General Practice (New York)
Minerva Med	Minerva Medica (Torino)
Minn Med	Minnesota Medicine (St. Paul)
Miss Med	Missouri Medicine (St. Louis)
Mo Med	Missouri Medicine (St. Louis)
Mod Health Care	Modern Health Care (New York)
Mod Nurs Home	Modern Nursing Home (Chicago)
Mod Treatm	Modern Treatment (New York)
Monist	Monist (La Salle, Illinois)
Munch Med Wochenschr or Munchen Med Wschr	Munchener Medizinische Wochenschrift
N Car Med J	North Carolina Medical Journal (North Carolina)
N S Med Bull	Nova Scotia Medical Bulletin (Halifax)
NM	Nurs Mirror and Midwives' Journal (London)
Nat Assn Women Deans & Couns J	National Association of Women Deans and Sounselors Journal (Washington)
Nat Par Teach	National Parent Teachers Bulletin (Chicago)
Nat R	National Review (New York)
Nation	Nation (New York)
Nation's Sch	Nation's Schools (Chicago)
Neb Med J	Nebraska State Medical Journal (Lincoln)
Ned Tidjdschr Genees- kd	Nederlands Tijdschrift voor Geneeskunde (Amsterdam)
New Cath World	New Catholic World (New York)
New Eng J Med	New England Journal of Medicine (Boston)
New Phys	New Physician (Flossmoor, Illinois)
New Republic	New Republic (Washington)
New Statesman	New Statesman (London)
New York Times	New York Times (New York)
Newsweek	Newsweek (New York)
Nicaragua Med	Nicaragua Medica (Managua)
Nord Med	Nordisk Medicin (Stockholm)
Nord Psykiat T	Nordisk Psykiatrisk Tidsskrift (Middlefart)
Northwest Med or NW Med	Northwest Medicine (Seattle)
Nouv Presse Med	Nouvelle Presse Medicale (Paris)
Nurs Care	Nursing Care (New York)

Nurs Clin N Amer	Nursing Clinics of North America (Philadelphia)
Nurs Forum	Nursing Forum (Chicago)
Nurs Homes	Nursing Homes (Washington)
Nurs Mirror or NM	Nursing Mirror and Midwives' Journal (London)
Nurs Outlk	Nursing Outlook (New York)
Nurs Res	Nursing Research (New York)
Nurs Res Conf	Nursing Research Conference (New York)
Nurs Res Rep	Nursing Research Report (New York)
Nurs Sci	Nursing Science (New York)
Nurs Times or NT	Nursing Times (London)
Nurs Update	Nursing Update (Greenwich, Connecticut)
Nurs J Singapore	Nursing Journal of Singapore (Singapore)
Nurs '73,'74	Nursing '3, '74 (Jenkintown, Pennsylvania)
N Y Hill Hosp J	New York Hillside Hospital Journal (New York)
N Y State J Med	New York State Journal of Medicine (New York)
N Y State Nurs Ass	New York State Nursing Association Journal (Albany)
NZ Nurs J	New Zealand Nursing Journal (Wellington, New Zealand)
Oh St Med J	Ohio State Medical Journal (Columbus)
Okla Nurs	Oklahoma Nurse (Oklahoma City, Oklahoma)
OR Reporter	OR Reporter (Southfield, Massachusetts)
Orv Hetil	Orvoosi Hetilap (Budapest)
Osteo Hosp	Osteopathic Hospital (Park Ridge, Illinois)
PN or Pract Nurs	Practical Nursing (New York)
Parents Mag	Parents' Magazine and Better Family Living (New York)
Past Psych	Pastoral Psychology (New York)
Pastoral Care	Pastoral Care and Counseling Abstracts (Richmond, Virginia)
Pediat Akush Ginekol	Pediatriia Akushertov i Ginekologiia (Kiev)
Pediat Clin N Am	Pediatric Clinics of North America (Philadelphia)
Pediat Curr	Pediatric Currents (New York)
Pediatrics	Pediatrics (Springfield, Illinois

Pediatriia	Pediatriia (Napoli)
Penn Med	Pennsylvania Medicine (Lemoyne, Pennsylvania)
Penn Nurs	Pennsylvania Nurse (Harrisburg, Pennsylvania)
Percept Mot Skills	Perceptual and Motor Skills (Missoula, Montana)
Perspect Psychiat Care	Perspectives in Psychiatric Care (Hillsdale, New Jersey)
Perspectivas	Perspectivas (Madrid)
Phi Delta Kappan	Phi Delta Kappan (Bloomington, Indiana)
Phillipp J Nurs	Phillippine Journal of Nursing (Manila)
Phys Ed	Physical Educator (Indianapolis)
Phys Man or Phys Manag	Physician's Management (Evanston, Illinois)
Phys Ther	Physical Therapy (New York)
Physician's Panorama	Physician's Panorama (Hanover, New Jersey)
Physiotherap	Physiotherapy (London)
Point View	Point of View (Somerville, New Jersey)
Pol Tyg Lek	Polski Tygodnik Lekarski (Warsaw)
Pop Sci	Popular Science (Boulder, Colorado)
Postgrad Med	Postgraduate Medicine (Minneapolis)
Postgrad Med J	Postgraduate Medical Journal (London)
Practitioner	Practitioner (London)
Prax Kinderpsychol	Praxis der Kinderpsychologie und Kinderpsychiatrie (Gottingen)
Praxis	Praxis (Bern)
Presse Med	Presse Medicale (Paris)
Prism	Prism (Chicago)
Prof Nurs Home	Professional Nursing Home (Minneapolis)
Proc Roy Soc Med	Proceedings of the Royal Society of Medicine (London)
Proc Rudolph Virchow	Proceedings of the Rudolph Virchow Society in the City of New York (New York)
Proc Staff Meet Mayo Clinic	Proceedings of the Staff Meetings of Mayo Clinic (Rochester)

Prose # 8	Prose # 8 (New York)
Prosth Dent	Journal of Prosthetic Dentistry (St. Louis)
Przegl Lek	Przeglad Lekarski (Cracow)
Psyche	Psyche (Heidelberg)
Psychiat & Soc Sc Rev	Psychiatry and Social Science Review (New York)
Psychiat Med	Psychiatry and Medical Practice Bulletin (Washington)
Psychiat Neural	Psychiatrisch Neurologisa e Washenschrift
Psychiat Res Rep Am Psychiat Ass	Psychiatric Research Reports of the American Psychiatric Association (Washington)
Psychiat Q	Psychiatric Quarterly (Utica)
Psychiatry	Psychiatry (Washington)
Psychoanal Rev	Psychoanalytic Review (New York)
Psychoanal Q	Psychoanalytic Quarterly (New York)
Psychoanalysis	Psychoanalysis and the Psychoanalytic Review (New York)
Psychoanalyt Study of the Child	Psychoanalytic Study of the Child (New York)
Psychol Bull	Psychological Bulletin (Washington)
Psychol Rep	Psychological Reports (Missoula, Montana)
Psychol Today	Psychology Today (New York)
Psychosom Med	Psychosomatic Medicine (New York)
Psychother Psychosom	Psychotherapy and Psychosomatics (Basel)
PT Care	Patient Care (Greenwich, Connecticut)
Public Health Rep	Public Health Reports (Washington)
Public Opinion	Public Opinion Quarterly (New York)
Public Svc Nurs Mag	Public Service Nursing Magazine (Washington)
Public Welfare	Public Welfare (Chicago)
Quart J Med	Quarterly Journal of Medicine (Oxford)
Queens Nurs	Queens Nursing Journal (London)

RN	Registered Nurse (New York)
RNABC News	Registered Nurses Association of British Columbia (Vancouver)
R Metaphys	Review of Metaphysics (New Haven, Connecticut)
Read Dig	Reader's Digest (Pleasantville)
Redbk	Redbook (New York)
Regan Rep Nurs Law	Regan Report on Nursing Law (Providence)
Relig Hea	Religious Health (New York)
Relig in Life	Religion in Life (Nashville)
Reporter	Reporter (Madison, Wisconsin)
Res Staff Phys	Resident & Staff Physician (Port Washington, New York)
Resp Care	Respiratory Care (Philadelphia)
Resusciation	Resusciation (London)
Rev Esp Anestesiol Reanim	Revista Espanola de Anestesiologia Reanimacion (Madrid)
Rev Fran Psychoanal or Rev Fr Psych	Revue Francaise de Psychanalys (Paris)
Rev Infirm	Revue de L'Infirmiere et de L'Assistante Sociale (Paris)
Rev Med Psychosom	Revue de Medicine Psychosomatique (Paris)
Rev Neuropsychiatr Infant	Revue de Neuropsychiatrie Infante et d'Hygiene Mentale de l'Enfance (Paris)
Rev Psicoanal	Revista de Psicoanalisis (Bueno Aries)
R I Med J	Rhode Island Medical Journal (Providence)
Rocky Mount Med J	Rocky Mountain Medical Journal (Denver)
Ruman Med Rev	Rumanian Medical Review (Bucharest)
SPCK	Society for Promoting Christian Knowledge (London)
SPEC	Spectator (Philadelphia)
SPEC	Spectator (London)
S A Nurs J	South African Nursing Journal (Pretoria)
S Afr Med J	South African Medical Journal (Capetown)
S Med J	Southern Medical Journal (Birmingham)

Safety Ed	Safety Education (Chicago)
Sairaanhoitaja	Sairaanhoitaja Sjukskoterskan (Helsinki)
Sat Eve Post	Saturday Evening Post (Philadelphia)
Sat R World	Saturday Review World (New York)
Sch Counsel	School Counselor (Washington)
Schweiz Arch Neurol Psychiat	Schweizer Archiv fur Neurologie Neurochirurgie und Psychiatri (Zurich)
Schweiz Z Psychol	Schweizerische Zeitschrift dur Psychologie (Zurich)
Schol Teacher/Jr/Sr High	Scholastic Teacher/ Junior-Senior High (New York)
Sci Am	Scientific American (New York)
Sci Dig	Scientific Digest (New York)
Sci N or Sci News Let	Science News Letter (Washington)
Science	Science (Washington)
Sem Hem	Seminars in Hematology (New York)
Sem Hop Inform	Semaine de Hopitaux de Paris, Informations (Paris)
Sem Hop Paris	Semaine des Hopitaux de Paris (Paris)
Semin Drug Treat	Seminars in Drug Treatment (New York)
Sing Med	Singapore Medical Journal (Singapore)
Soc Casework	Social Casework (New York)
Soc Forces	Social Forces (New York)
Soc Prob	Social Problems (New York)
Soc Psychol	Social Psychology (New York)
Soc Q	Social Quarterly (Columbia, Missouri)
Soc Res	Social Research (New York)
Soc Sci Med	Social Science and Medicine (Oxford)
Soc Work	Social Work Technique (Washington)
Sovet Zdravookhr	Sovetskoye Zdravookhraneniye (Moscow)
Statis Bull Metrop Life Ins Co	Statistical Bulletin of the Metropolitan Life Insurance Company (New York)
Stud Gen	Studium Generale (Berlin)

Superv Nurse	Supervisor Nurse (Chicago)
Surg Gynecol Obstet	Surgery, Gynecology, and Obstetrics (Chicago)
Surgery	Surgery (St. Louis)
Svensk Lakartidn	Svenska Lakartidningen (Stockholm)
Sykepleien	Sykepleien (Stockholm)
Symposium	Symposium: Group for the Advancement of Psychiatry (New York)
T Norsk Laegeforen	Tidskrift for den Norske Laegeforening (Oslo)
T Sygepl	Tidskrift Sygeplejersken (Oslo)
T Ziekenverpl	Tidjdschrift Voor Zienkenver-pleging (Amsterdam)
Teach	Teacher (Greenwich, Connecticut)
Tex Med	Texas Medicine (Austin)
Theol Today	Theology Today (Princeton)
Ther Umsch	Therapeutische Umschaw (Berlin)
Therap Recreation	Theraueutic Recreation Journal (Arlington, Virginia)
Tidskr Sver Sjukskot	Tidskrift for Sveriges Sjukskot-erskor (Stockholm)
Time	Time (Chicago)
Times Ed Suppl	Times Educational Supplement (London)
Today's Ed	Today's Education (Washington)
Today's Health	Today's Health (Chicago)
Tom Nurs	Tomorrow's Nurse (Nantucket, Massachusetts)
Trans Am Acad Opthal-mol Otolaryngol	Transactions: American Academy of Opthamology and Otolaryn-gology (Rochester, Minnesota)
Transaction	Transaction (New Brunswick, New Jersey)
Trauma	Trauma (New York)
Triangle	Triangle (Basel)
Tuberculology	Tuberculology (Denver)
Tufts Health Sci Rev	Tufts Health Science Review (Boston)
Turk J Pediatr	Turkish Journal of Pediatrics (Ankara)
Twentieth Cent	Twentieth Century (London)
Tx Rep Biol Med	Texas Reports on Biology and Medicine (Austin)
Ugeskr Laeger	Ugeskrift for Laeger (Copenhaven)
UNA Nurs J	UNA Nurses Journal (Melbourne)

Und Child	Understanding the Child (New York)
Urban Health	Urban Health (Atlanta)
Va Med Mo	Virginia Medical Monthly (Richmond)
Vie Med Can Fr	Vie Medicale au Canada France (Quebec)
Voenmed or Voennomed	Voenno-Med Itsinskii Zhurnal (Moscow)
Vol Lead	Volunteer Leader (Chicago)
W Med J or Wis Med J	Wisconsin Medical Journal (Madison)
Wash J Nurs	Washington State Journal of Nursing (Seattle)
Wash Post	Washington Post (Washington)
Wiad Lek	Wiadomosci Lekarskie (Warsaw)
Wien Med Wschr	Wiener Medizinische Wochen- schrift (Vienna)
Woman's Home C	Woman's Home Companion (Springfield, Ohio)
Yng Laeg	Yngre Laeger (Copenhaven)
Young Child	Young Children (Washington)
Z Allgemeinmed	Zettschrift fur Allgemeinmed- izin; der Landarzt (Stuttgart)
Z Klin Psychol Psycho- ther	Zeitschrift fur Klinische Psychologie und Psychotherapie (Munich)
Z Psychother Med Psychol	Zeitschrift fuer Psychotherapie und Medizinischr Psychologie (Stuttgart)
Zdravookhr Ross Fed	Zdravookhraneniye Rossiiskoi Federatzil (Moscow)
Zh Eksp Klin Med	Zhurnal Eksperimental noi i Klinischeskoi Meditsiny (Erevan) (Moscow)

Adolescents
Allied Health Services
Anxiety
Assassination
Attitudes Toward Death:
  Adolescents
Attitudes Toward Death:
  Allied Health Services
Attitudes Toward Death:
  Anxiety
Attitudes Toward Death:
  Assassinations
Attitudes Toward Death:
  Cancer Patients
Attitudes Toward Death:
  Coronary Care Patients
Attitudes Toward Death:
  Depression
Attitudes Toward Death:
  Emotion
Attitudes Toward Death:
  Execution
Attitudes Toward Death:
  Fear of Death
Attitudes Toward Death:
  Fear of the Dead
Attitudes Toward Death:
  General
Attitudes Toward Death:
  Geriatrics
Attitudes Toward Death:
  Giving Up
Attitudes Toward Death:
  Individuals
Attitudes Toward Death:
  Measurement
Attitudes Toward Death:
  Mentally Ill People
Attitudes Toward Death:
  Nurses
Attitudes Toward Death:
  Nursing Aides
Attitudes Toward Death:
  Nursing Students

Attitudes Toward Death:
  Other Cultures
Attitudes Toward Death:
  Physicians
Attitudes Toward Death:
  Reactions
Attitudes Toward Death:
  Religion
Attitudes Toward Death:
  Sense of Dying
Attitudes Toward Death:
  Sex Differences
Attitudes Toward Death:
  Time Sense
Bereavement: Bibliography
  on
Bereavement: Children
Bereavement: Counseling
Bereavement: Dentist
Bereavement: Family
Bereavement: General
Bereavement: Geriatrics
Bereavement: Other
  Cultures
Bereavement: Parents
Bereavement: Pets
Bereavement:
  Psychiatric Aspects
Bereavement:
  Social Aspects
Bereavement:
  Transplant Patients
Bereavement:
  University Students
Bereavement:
  Widows and Widowers
Cancer:
  Attitudes of Patients
Cancer:
  Attitudes of Physicians
Cancer: Awareness of
Cancer: Care
Cancer: Children
Cancer: Counseling

TABLE OF CONTENTS

BOOKS

Abrahamsson, H. THE ORIGIN OF DEATH: STUDIES IN
AFRICAN MYTHOLOGY. Uppsala: Studia Ethnographica
Upsaliensia, 3, 1951.

Aldwinckle, R. F. DEATH IN THE SECULAR CITY. London:
G. Allen, 1972. Also published by: Grand Rapids,
Michigan: William B. Eerdmans Publishing Co., 1974.

Allen, D. FINDING OUR FATHER. Richmond, Virginia:
John Knox Press, 1974.

Anthony, Sylvia. DISCOVERY OF DEATH IN CHILDHOOD
AND AFTER. New York: Basic Books, 1972.

Aries, P. WESTERN ATTITUDES TOWARD DEATH. Baltimore:
Johns Hopkins University Press, 1974.

Arnstein, Helene S. WHAT TO TELL YOUR CHILD ABOUT BIRTH,
ILLNESS, DEATH, DIVORCE, AND OTHER FAMILY CRISES.
Indianapolis: The Bobbs-Merrill Co., 1960.

Bayly, J. T. THE VIEW FROM A HEARSE. Elgin, Illinois:
D. C. Cook, 1973.

Becker. E. THE DENIAL OF DEATH. New York: Collier-
Macmillan, 1973.

Bell, T. IN THE MIDST OF LIFE. New York: Atheneum,
1961.

Bender, David. L., ed. PROBLEMS OF DEATH: OPPOSING
VIEWPOINTS. Anoka, Minnesota: Greenhaven, 1974.

Bermann, Eric. SCAPEGOAT: THE IMPACT OF A DEATH ON AN
AMERICAN FAMILY. Ann Arbor, Michigan: University of
Michigan Press, 1973.

Bowlby, J. ATTACHMENT AND LOSS. New York: Basic Books,
1969.

Brim, O., et al. THE DYING PATIENT. New York: Russell
Sage Foundation, 1970.

Bro, Marguerite H. WHEN CHILDREN ASK. New York:
Harper and Brothers, 1956.

Budge, E. A. Wallis. THE BOOK OF THE DEAD. New Hyde
Park, New York: University Books, Inc., 1960.

Caine, Lynn. WIDOW. New York: Morrow, 1974.

Cancer Care, Inc. THE IMPACT, COSTS, AND CONSEQUENCES
OF A CATASTROPHIC ILLNESS ON PATIENTS AND FAMILIES:
A REPORT OF A SOCIAL RESEARCH STUDY OF SELECTED FAMILIE
STRICKEN BY ADVANCED CANCER. New York: Cancer Care,
Inc., 1973.

Carlozzi, Carl. G. DEATH AND CONTEMPORARY MAN. Grand
Rapids, Michigan, William B. Eerdmans Publishing Co.,
1968.

Cartwright, Ann, et al. LIFE BEFORE DEATH. Boston:
Routledge and Kegan, 1973.

Choron, Jacques. DEATH AND MODERN MAN. New York:
Collier Books, 1971.

--- DEATH AND WESTERN THOUGHT. New York: Collier Books,
1963.

---MODERN MAN AND MORTALITY. New York: Macmillan, 1964.

Cornils, Stanley. MANAGING GRIEF WISELY. Grand Rapids,
Michigan: Baker Books, 1967.

Crane, Diana. SOCIAL ASPECTS OF THE PROLONGATION OF
LIFE. New York: Russell Sage Foundation, 1969.

Cutter, F. COMING TO TERMS WITH DEATH: HOW TO FACE
THE INEVITABLE WITH WISDOM AND DIGNITY. Chicago:
Nelson-Hall, 1974.

de Padvillez, A. JOY IN THE FACE OF DEATH. New York:
Desclee, 1963.

Doss, R. W. THE LAST ENEMY. New York: Harper, 1974.

Dumont, R. G., et al. THE AMERICAN VIEW OF DEATH:
ACCEPTANCE OR DENIAL? Cambridge, Massachussetts:
Schenkman, 1972.

Easson, William M. DYING CHILD: THE MANAGEMENT OF THE
CHILD OR ADOLESCENT WHO IS DYING. Springfield,
Illinois: C. C. Thomas, 1972.

Eissler, K. R. THE PSYCHIATRIST AND THE DYING PATIENT.
New York: International Universities Press, 1955.

Elliot, G. TWENTIETH CENTURY BOOK OF THE DEAD. New
York: Scribner, 1972.

Ellison, J. THE LAST THIRD OF LIFE CLUB. Philadelphia:
United Church Press, 1973.

Eshelman, Byron. DEATH ROW CHAPLAIN Englewood Cliffs,
New Jersey: Prentice Hall, 1962.

Ettinger, Robert C. W. THE PROSPECT OF IMMORTALITY.
Garden City, New York: Doubleday, 1964.

Evans, Jocelyn. LIVING WITH A MAN WHO IS DYING. New
York: Taplinger, 1971.

Fassler, J. MY GRANDPA DIED TODAY. New York: Behavioral
Publications, 1971.

Feifel, Herman. THE MEANING OF DEATH. New York: McGraw
Hill, 1959.

Fortune, Dion. THROUGH THE GATES OF HELL. Hackensack,
New Jersey: Wehman, 1968.

Foundation of Thanatology. BEREAVEMENT AND ILLNESS.
New York: H S Publishing Corp., 1973.

Fraser, J. T. THE VOICES OF TIME: A COOPERATIVE SURVEY
OF MAN'S VIEW OF TIME AS EXPRESSED BY THE SCIENCES
AND BY THE HUMANITIES. New York: George Braziller,
1966.

Fulton, Robert. DEATH AND IDENTITY. New York: Wiley,
1965.

---THE SACRED AND THE SECULAR: ATTITUDES OF THE AMERICAN
PUBLIC TOWARD DEATH. Milwaukee: Bulfin, 1963.

Furman, E. A CHILD'S PARENT DIES. New Haven: Yale
University Press, 1974.

Gengerelli, J. A., et al., eds. PSYCHOLOGICAL FACTORS
IN HUMAN CANCER. Berkeley: University of California
Press, 1953.

Gerard, H. I., THE RELATIONSHIP BETWEEN RELIGIOUS
BELIEF AND DEATH AFFECT. Princeton, New Jersey:
Princeton University Press, 1958.

Gittelsohn, Roland B. MAN'S BEST HOPE. New York: Random
House, 1961.

Glaser, Barney, et al. AWARENESS OF DYING. Chicago:
Aldine Publishing Co., 1965.

--- TIME FOR DYING. Chicago: Aldine Publishing Co.,
1968.

Goldberg, et al., eds. MEDICAL CARE OF THE DYING
PATIENT. New York: H. S. Publishing Corp., 1973.

Gordon, David C. OVERCOMING THE FEAR OF DEATH. New
York: Macmillan, 1970.

Gorer, Geoffrey. DEATH, GRIEF, AND MOURNING. Garden
City, New York: Doubleday, 1965. Also published by:
London: Cresset Press, 1965.

Green, Betty, et al. DEATH EDUCATION: PREPARATION FOR
LIVING. Cambridge, Massachussets: Schenkman, 1971.

Grollman, E. A., ed. CONCERNING DEATH: A PRACTICAL GUIDE
FOR THE LIVING. Boston: Beacon Press, 1974.

4

---EXPLAINING DEATH TO CHILDREN. Boston: Beacon Press, 1967.

Group for the Advancement of Psychiatry Conference. DEATH AND DYING: ATTITUDES OF PATIENT AND DOCTOR: PROCEEDINGS, VOLUME 5 (SYMPOSIUM NUMBER 11). New York: Group for the Advancement of Psychiatry, 1965.

Harrington, A. THE IMMORTALIST. London: Panther Books, 1973.

Hendin, D. DEATH AS A FACT OF LIFE. New York: Warner Paperback Library, 1974. Also published by: New York: Norton, 1973.

Hertz, Robert. DEATH AND THE RIGHT HAND. Aberdeen, England: University Press, 1960.

Herzog, Edgar. PSYCHE AND DEATH. New York: Putnam, 1967. Also published by: London: Hodger and Stoughton, Ltd., 1966.

Hess, Marlene. WHAT YOU SHOULD KNOW ABOUT DEATH. New Canaan, Connecticut: Keats Publishing, 1974.

Hinton, John. DYING. Baltimore: Penguin, 1967.

Hocking, William Ernest. THE MEANING OF IMMORTALITY IN HUMAN EXPERIENCE. New York: Harper and Row, 1957. Also published by: Westport, Connecticut: Greenwood Press, 1973.

Hoffman, Frederick John. THE MORTAL NO: DEATH AND THE MODERN IMAGINATION. Princeton, New Jersey: Princeton University Press, 1964.

Holbrook, David. HUMAN HOPE AND THE DEATH INSTINCT: AN EXPLORATION OF PSYCHOANALYTICAL THEORIES OF HUMAN NATURE AND THEIR IMPLICATIONS FOR CULTURE AND EDUCA- TION. Elmsford, New York: Pergamon, 1971.

Hughes, H. L. G. PEACE AT THE LAST. London: Calouste Gulbenkian Foundation, 1960.

Institute of Medicine of Chicago. TERMINAL CARE FOR CANCER PATIENTS. Chicago: Institute of Medicine of Chicago, 1950.

Jackson, Edgar N. FOR THE LIVING. New York: Channel
Press, 1965.

---TELLING A CHILD ABOUT DEATH. New York: Channel
Press, 1965.

---UNDERSTANDING GRIEF. New York: Abingdon Press, 1957.

Joint National Cancer Survey Committee. REPORT ON A
NATIONAL SURVEY CONCERNING PATIENTS WITH CANCER
NURSED AT HOME. London: Marie Curie Memorial, 1952.

Kastenbaum, Robert, et al. THE PSYCHOLOGY OF DEATH.
New York: Springer, 1972.

Kavanaugh, R. E. FACING DEATH. Los Angeles, California:
Nash, 1972. Also published by: Baltimore: Penguin,
1974.

Klein, S. THE FINAL MYSTERY. Garden City, New York:
Doubleday, 1974.

Krant, M. J. DYING AND DIGNITY: THE MEANING AND CONTROL
OF A PERSONAL DEATH. Springfield, Illinois: C. C.
Thomas, 1974.

Kreis, Bernadine. UP FROM GRIEF. New York: Seabury
Press, 1969.

Kubler-Ross, E. ON DEATH AND DYING. New York: Macmillan,
1969.

---QUESTIONS AND ANSWERS ON DEATH AND DYING. New York:
Collier Books, 1974.

Kutscher, Austin H., et al. BIBLIOGRAPHY OF BOOKS ON
DEATH, BEREAVEMENT, LOSS AND GRIEF: 1935 -1968.
Burbank, California: Health Sciences Publishing Corp.,
1969.

---ed. BUT NOT TO LOSE -- A BOOK OF COMFORT FOR THOSE
BEREAVED. New York: Fell, 1969.

--- et al. CARING FOR THE DYING PATIENT AND HIS FAMILY.
New York: H. S. Publishing Corporation, 1973.

---DEATH AND BEREAVEMENT. Springfield, Illinois: C.C.
Thomas, 1969.

--- et al. ORAL CARE OF THE AGING AND DYING PATIENT.
Springfield, Illinois: C. C. Thomas, 1969.

---RELIGION AND BEREAVEMENT. New York: H. S. Publishing
Corporation, 1972.

---PSYCHOPHARMACOLOGIC AGENTS IN THE CARE OF THE TERM-
INALLY ILL AND THE BEREAVED. n.p. Foundation of
Thanatology, 1973.

--- THE TERMINAL PATIENT:ORAL CARE. New York: Columbia
University Press, 1973.

Lamm, M. THE JEWISH WAY IN DEATH AND MOURNING. New
York: J. David, 1972.

Landsberg, P. L. EXPERIENCE OF DEATH. New York:
Philosophical Library, 1953.

Lee, J. Y. DEATH AND BEYOND IN THE EASTERN PERSPECTIVE.
New York: Gordon and Breach, 1974.

Lepp, Ignace. DEATH AND ITS MYSTERIES. New York: Macmillan, 1968.

Levin, Sidney, et al. PSYCHODYNAMIC STUDIES ON AGING:
CREATIVITY, REMINISCING AND DYING. New York: International Universities Press, 1967.

Lifton, Robert Jay, et al. LIVING AND DYING. New
York: Prager, 1974.

Lowry, Richard James. MALE-FEMALE DIFFERENCES IN
ATTITUDES TOWARD DEATH. (Ph. D. Dissertation)
Waltham, Massachussetts: Brandeis University, 1965.

Mannes, Marya. LAST RIGHTS, A CASE FOR THE GOOD DEATH.
New York: Morrow, 1973.

Marks, E. SIMONE DE BEAUVOIR: ENCOUNTERS WITH DEATH.
New Brunswick, New Jersey: Rutgers University Press,
1973.

Marris, Peter. WIDOWS AND THEIR FAMILIES. London:
    Routledge & Kegan Paul, 1958.

McGeachy, D. P. MATTER OF LIFE AND DEATH. Richmond,
    Virginia: John Knox Press, 1966.

Miller, R. C. LIVE UNTIL YOU DIE. Philadelphia:
    United Church Press, 1973.

Mitchell, Marjorie Editha. THE CHILD'S ATTITUDE TO
    DEATH. New York: Schocken Books, Inc., 1967.

Mitford, Jessica. THE AMERICAN WAY OF DEATH. New
    York: Simon and Schuster, 1963.

Mohr, G. J. WHEN CHILDREN FACE CRISES. Chicago: Spencer
    Press, Inc., 1952.

Moriarty, David M. LOSS OF LOVED ONES: THE EFFECTS OF A
    DEATH IN THE FAMILY ON PERSONALITY DEVELOPMENT.Spring-
    field, Illinois: C. C. Thomas, 1967.

Munnichs, J. M. A. OLD AGE AND FINITUDE. White Plains,
    New York: A. J. Phiebig, 1966.

National Association of Social Workers. HELPING THE
    DYING PATIENT AND HIS FAMILY. New York: National
    Association of Social Workers, 1960.

Neale, R. E. THE ART OF DYING. New York: Harper, 1973.

Newman, Eric. DEATH PSYCHOLOGY AND THE NEW ETHIC. New
    York: Harper and Row, 1973.

Osborne, E. WHEN YOU LOSE A LOVED ONE. New York: Public
    Affairs Committee, 1958.

PASTORAL CARE OF THE DYING AND THE BEREAVED: SELECTED
    READINGS. New York: Health Sciences Publishing
    Corporation, 1973.

Pearson, Leonard, ed. DEATH AND DYING: CURRENT ISSUES
    IN THE TREATMENT OF THE DYING PERSON. Cleveland:
    Case Western Reserve University Press, 1969.

PROCEEDINGS: DEATH AND ATTITUDES TOWARD DEATH. University of Minnesota Medical School, 1972.

PSYCHIATRY AND THE INTERNIST. New York: Grune and Stratton, Inc., 1970.

PSYCHOSOCIAL ASPECTS OF TERMINAL CARE. New York: Columbia University Press, 1972.

Quint, J. C. THE NURSE AND THE DYING PATIENT. New York: Macmillan, 1967.

Rabinowicz, H. A. A GUIDE TO LIFE, JEWISH LAWS AND CUSTOMS OF MOURNING. London: Jewish Chronicle Publications, 1964.

Reed, E. L. HELPING CHILDREN WITH THE MYSTERIES OF DEATH. Nashville: Abingdon, 1970.

Rheingold, J. THE MOTHER, ANXIETY, AND DEATH: THE CATASTROPHIC DEATH COMPLEX. Boston: Little, Brown and Co., 1967.

Rolansky, John D., ed. THE END OF LIFE. New York: Fleet Press Corporation, 1973.

Ruitenbeek, Hendrik M. THE INTERPRETATION OF DEATH. n.p.: J. Aronson, 1973.

Saunders, C. CARE OF THE DYING. London: Macmillan, 1959.

Schoenberg, Bernard, et al. ANTICIPATORY GRIEF. New York: Columbia University Press, 1974.

---LOSS AND GRIEF: PSYCHOLOGICAL MANAGEMENT IN MEDICAL PRACTICE. New York: Columbia University Press, 1970.

---PSYCHOSOCIAL ASPECTS OF TERMINAL CARE. New York: Columbia University Press, 1972.

---TERMINAL PATIENT: ORAL CARE. New York: Columbia University Press, 1973.

Segerberg, O. THE IMMORTALITY FACTOR. New York: Dutton, 1974.

Sellin, Thorsten, ed. CAPITAL PUNISHMENT. New York: Harper and Row, 1967.

Shepard, Martin. SOMEONE YOU LOVE IS DYING: A GUIDE FOR HELPING AND COPING. New York: Harmony Books,1975.

Sherrill, Helen H., et al. INTERPRETING DEATH TO CHILD REN. New York: National Council of the Churches of Christ, 1956.

Shibles, Warren. DEATH: AN INTERDISCIPLINARY ANALYSIS. Whitewater, Wisconsin: Language Press, 1974.

Shneidman, Edwin S. DEATH AND THE COLLEGE STUDENT. New York: Behavioral Publications, 1972.

---THE DEATHS OF MAN. New York: Quadrangle, 1973.

---ESSAYS IN SELF-DESTRUCTION. New York: SCience House, 1967.

Smith, Helen C. CARE OF THE DYING PATIENT:A COMPARISON OF INSTRUCTIONAL PLANS. Bloomington, Indiana: Indiana University Press, 1965.

Stephens, S. DEATH COMES HOME. New York: Morehouse-Barlow, 1973.

Stringfellow, W. INSTEAD OF DEATH. New York: Seabury Press, 1963.

Sudnow, D. PASSING ON: THE SOCIAL ORGANIZATION OF DYING. Englewood Cliffs, New Jersey: Prentice Hall, 1967.

Taves, I. LOVE MUST NOT BE WASTED. New York: Crowell, 1974.

Taylor, M. J.,ed. THE MYSTERY OF SUFFERING AND DEATH. Staten Island, New York: Alba House, 1973.

Toynbee, A., et al. MAN'S CONCERN WITH DEATH. New York: McGraw-Hill Book Co., 1968.

Troup, Stanley B., et al.,eds.PATIENT, DEATH, AND THE FAMILY. New York: Scribner, 1974.

Ulanov, B. DEATH: A BOOK OF PREPARATION AND CONSOLATION.
New York: Sheed and Ward, 1959.

United States Senate. Committee on Labor and Public
Welfare. Subcommittee on Health. MEDICAL ETHICS:
THE RIGHT TO SURVIVAL. Washington: GPO, 1974.

--- Special Committee on Aging. DEATH WITH DIGNITY: AN
INQUIRY INTO RELATED PUBLIC ISSUES: HEARINGS. Washington: GPO, 1972.

Vernick, J. SELECTED BIBLIOGRAPHY ON DEATH AND DYING.
Washington: Information Office, National Institute
of Child Health and Human Development, U. S. Depart-
ment of Health, Education, and Welfare, 1971.

Verwoerdt, Adriaan. COMMUNICATION WITH THE FATALLY
ILL. Springfield, Illinois: C. C. Thomas, 1966.

Warner, W. L. THE LIVING AND THE DEAD. New Haven,
Connecticut: Yale University Press, 1959.

Weisman, A. D. ON DEATH AND DYING: A PSYCHIATRIC STUDY
OF TERMINALITY. New York: Behavioral Publications,
1972.

---THE EXISTENTIAL CORE OF PSYCHOANALYSIS: REALITY SENSE
AND RESPONSIBILITY. Boston: Little, Brown and Co.,
1965.

Wertenbaker, Lael T. DEATH OF A MAN. New York: Random
House, 1957.

WHEN YOU LOSE A LOVED ONE. New York: Public Affairs
Pamphlet, 1958.

Williams, R., et al. , eds. PROCESS OF AGING: SOCIAL
AND PSYCHOLOGICAL PERSPECTIVES. (2 vols.) New York:
Atherton Press, 1963.

Wolf, Anna W. M. HELPING YOUR CHILD TO UNDERSTAND DEATH.
New York: Child Study Association, 1958.

Wolfenstein, M., et al. CHILDREN AND THE DEATH OF A
PRESIDENT. Garden City, New York: Doubleday, 1966.

11

Zeligs, R. CHILDREN'S EXPERIENCE WITH DEATH. Springfield, Illinois: C. C. Thomas, 1974.

Zinker, Joseph Chaim, et al. ROSA LEE: MOTIVATION
AND THE CRISIS OF DYING. n.p.: Lake Erie College
Press, 1966.

PERIODICAL LITERATURE

SUBJECT INDEX

ADOLESCENTS
SEE ALSO: CHILDREN
"The Adolescent Patient's Decision to Die," by J. E.
  Schowalter, et al. PEDIATRICS 51:97-103, January,
  1973.

"Adolescent Attitudes Toward Death," by A. Maurer.
  J GENET PSYCHOL 105:75-90, September, 1964.

"Adolescent Views of Death," by R. A. Hogan.
  ADOLESCENCE 5:55-66, Spring, 1970.

"Affective Responses to the Concept of Death in a
  Population of Children and Early Adolescents," by
  I. E. Alexander, et al. J GENET PSYCHOL 93:167-177.
  1958.

"Attitudes Toward Death and Future Life Among Normal
  and Subnormal Adolescent Girls," by C. L. Stacey,
  et al. EXCEP CHILD 20:259-262, March, 1954.

"Coping Behaviors of Fatally Ill Adolescents and
  Their Parents," by J. S. Lowenberg. NURS FORUM
  9:269-287, No. 3, 1970.

"Denial of Death and the Unconscious Longing for In-
  destructability and Immortality in the Terminal
  Phase of Adolescence," by G. J. Sarwer-Foner.
  CAN PSYCHIATR ASSOC J 17:Suppl 2:SS51, 1972.

"Dying of the Young," by J. Boger. HOSP HEALTH CARE
  ADMIN 3:14-17, June, 1973.

"A Leukemic Adolescent's Verbalization About Dying,"
  by J. Kikuchi. MATERN CHILD NURS J 1:259-264, Fall,
  1973.

ADOLESCENTS

"Meeting the Needs of the Adolescent Patient," by
A. Jacobson. J PRACT NURS 20:39, October, 1970.

"Mileau Design for Adolescents with Lukemia," by J.
Vernick, et al. AMER J NURS 67:559-561, March,
1967.

"Primitive Concepts of Death and Rebirth in Two
Adolescents," by A. H. Green. PSYCHIAT QUART
(Suppl) 38:21-31, 1964.

"A Terminally Ill Adolescent and Her Family," by
M. B. Maxwell. AM J NURS 72:925-927, May, 1972.

ALLIED HEALTH SERVICES
"Attitudes of Physical Therapists Toward Death and
Terminal Illness," by C. A. Lutticken, et al.
PHYS THERAPY 54:226-32, March, 1974.

"Attitudes Toward Death Among Nursing Home Personnel,"
by J. Pearlman, et al. J GENET PSYCHOL 114:63-75,
March, 1969.

"Don't Mention It: The Physical Therapist in a
Death-Denying Society," by R. B. Purtilo. PHYS
THER 52:1031-1035, October, 1972.

"Effect of Work Experience in a Nursing Home on the
Attitudes Toward Death Held by Nursing Aides," by
E. Howard. GERONTOLOGIST 14:54-56, February, 1974.

"Family and Staff During Last Weeks and Days of
Terminal Illness," by A. Strauss ANN NY ACAD SCI
164:687-695, December 19, 1969.

"The Funeral of a Psychiatric Aide," by R. A. Schmie-
deck. BULL MENNINGER CLIN 36:641-645, November,
1972.

"Geriatric Staff Attitudes Toward Death," by D. S.
Kazzaz, et al. J AMER GERIAT SOC 16:1364-1371,
December, 1968.

"Living with the Dying: Weekly Therapy Group for Staff
Members Who Regularly Care for The Terminally Ill,"
NEWSWEEK 84:89, December 2, 1974.

ALLIED HEALTH SERVICES

"Philosophical or Psychological? The Physiological
   Process of Dying -- A Physiologist Looks at Death,"
   by E. Brown, Jr. J KANSAS MED SOC 68:127-128, March,
   1967.

"Physiotherapy and the Care of the Progressively Ill
   Patient. 1. The Role of the Physiotherapist," by
   P. A. Downie NURS TIMES 69:892-893, July 12, 1973.

"Role of Paramedical Staff with the Dying Patient,"
   by B. Newman. THERAP RECREATION J 8:29-33, No. 1,
   1974.

"Role of the Recreation Therapist with the Terminally
   Ill Child," by B. M. Lovelace. THERAP RECREATION
   J 8:25-28, No. 1, 1974.

"Utilizing Allied Health Personnel in the Management
   of Death," PT CARE 4:81+. May 31, 1970.

"Volunteers Bring Comfort and Hope to the Critically
   Ill," by M. A. Culp. VOLUNTEER LEADER 13:10-12,
   November, 1972.

"What is a Physical Therapist's Role in Treating a
   Dying Patient?" by M. Miller, et al. PHYS THERAPY
   53:325-326, March, 1973.

ANXIETY
   SEE ATTITUDES TOWARD DEATH: ANXIETY

ASSASSINATION
   SEE ATTITUDES TOWARD DEATH: ASSASSINATION

ATTITUDES TOWARD DEATH:ADOLESCENTS
   SEE ADOLESCENTS

ATTITUDES TOWARD DEATH: ALLIED HEALTH SERVICES

ATTITUDES TOWARD DEATH: ANXIETY
   "Anxiety and Two Cognitive Forms of Resistance to the
   Idea of Death," by S. L. Golding, et al. PSYCHOL
   REP 18:359-364, April, 1966.

ATTITUDES TOWARD DEATH: ANXIETY

"Anxiety as an Aid in the Prognostication of Impending Death," by J. S. Beigler. AM MED ASSN
ARCH NEUR AND PATH 77:171-177, 1957.

"Castration Anxiety and the Fear of Death," by
I. Sarnoff, et al. J PERSONAL 27:374-385,
September, 1959.

"The Construction and Validation of a Death
Anxiety Scale," by D. I. Templer. J GEN PSYCHOL
82:165-177, April, 1970.

"Curvilinearity Between Dream Content and Death
Anxiety and the Relationship of Death Anxiety to
Repression-Sensitization," by P. J. Handal, et al.
J ABNORM PSYCHOL 77:11-16, February, 1971.

"Death Anxiety and the Primal Scene," by D. B.
Friedman PSYCHOANALYSIS 48:108-118, Winter, 1961-
1962.

"Death Anxiety as Related to Depression and Health
of Retired Persons," by D. I. Templer. J GERONTOL
26:521-523, October, 1971.

"An MMPI Scale for Assessing Death Anxiety," by D.
I. Templer, et al. PSYCHOL REP 34:238, February,
1974.

"The Relationship Between Subjective Life Expectancy ,
Death Anxiety and General Anxiety," by P. J. Handal
J CLIN PSYCHOL 25:39-42, January, 1969.

"Religious Correlates of Death Anxiety," by D. I.
Templer, et al. PSYCHOL REP 26:895-897, June, 1970.

"Separation Anxiety," by John Bowlby INT J PSYCHO
41:89-113, 1960.

ATTITUDES TOWARD DEATH: ASSASSINATION
"The Assassination of President Kennedy:A Preliminary
Report on Public Reactions and Behavior," by Paul
B. Sheatsley, et al. PUBLIC OPINION Q 28: 189-
215, 1964.

ATTITUDES TOWARD DEATH: ASSASSINATIONS

"The Day the President Was Assassinated: Patient's
Reaction in One Mental Hospital," by R. V. Heckel
MENT HOSP 15:48, January, 1964.

"The Death of a President: Reactions of Psychoanalytic Patients," by D. Kirschner BEHAV SCI
10:1-6, January, 1965.

"The Influence of Death Upon Hero-Identification
Among Psychiatric Patients," by W. R. Bartz
J SOC PSYCHOL 76: 249-251, December, 1968.

ATTITUDES TOWARD DEATH: CANCER PATIENTS
SEE CANCER

ATTITUDES TOWARD DEATH: CORONARY CARE PATIENTS
"Adaptation to Open Heart Surgery: A Psychiatric
Study of Response to the Threat of Death," by
H. S. Abrams AM J PSYCHIAT 122:659-667, 1965.

"Death Fear in Dying Heart and Cancer Patients,"
by H. Feifel, et al. J PSYCHOSOM RES 17:161-166,
July, 1973.

"Emotional Reactions to the Threat of Impending
Death. A Study of Patients on the Monitor
Cardiac Pacemaker," by I. W. Browne, et al. IRISH
J MED SCI 6:177-187, April, 1967.

"How Coronary Patients Respond to Last Rites," by
N. H. Cassem, et al. POST GRAD MED 45:147-152,
1969.

"Patients' Reactions to Death in a Coronary Care
Unit," by J. G. Bruhn, et al. J PSYCHOSOM RES
14:65-70, March, 1970.

"Psychological Aspects of Sudden Cardiac Death,"
by F. G. Surawicz HEART AND LUNG 2:836-840,
November-December, 1973.

ATTITUDES TOWARD DEATH: DEPRESSION
"Critique of 'Denial and Depression'," by R. H.
Vispo PSYCHIATR Q 45:405-409, 1971.

ATTITUDES TOWARD DEATH: DEPRESSION

"Depression in Relation to Early and Recent Parent Death," by J. Birtchnell BRIT J PSYCHIAT 116:299-306, March, 1970.

ATTITUDES TOWARD DEATH: EMOTION
"Emotional Adjustment in Terminal Patients: A Quantitative Approach," by R. G. Carey J COUNSEL PSYCHOL 21:433-439, September, 1974.

"Emotional Reactions Associated with Death," by J. Ellard MED J AUST 1:979-983, June, 1968.

"Emotional Reactions to Death and Suicide," by J. H. Masserman AM PRACT & DIGEST TREAT (Supp.) 5:41-46, November, 1954.

"The Sadness of the Dying Patient," by C. K. Aldrich NICARAGUA MED 19:177-183, July-August, 1963.

"Some Correlates of Thoughts and Feelings Concerning Death," I. M. Greenberg, et al. J HILLSIDE HOSP 11: 120-126, April-July 1962.

ATTITUDES TOWARD DEATH: EXECUTION
"The Deterrent Influence of the Death Penalty," by K. F. Schuessler ANNALS OF AM ACAD OF POL & SOC SCI 284:54-62, 1952.

"More Than One Execution: Who Goes First?" by D. Lester, et al. JAMA 217:215, July 12, 1971.

"Reaction to Extreme Stress: Impending Death by Execution," by H. Bluestone, et al. AM J PSYCHIAT 119:393-396, November, 1962.

"Stay of Execution: Excerpts," by S. Alsop SAT R WORLD 1:20-23, December 18, 1973.

ATTITUDES TOWARD DEATH: FEAR OF DEATH
"The Apprehensive Patient," by S. Powers, et al. AJN 67:58+, January, 1967.

"Attempt at the Psychological Analysis of the Fear of Death," by S. Biran CONFIN PSYCHIAT 11:154-176, 1968.

"Biotrauma, Fear of Death and Agression," by M. M.
   Stern INT J PSYCHOANAL 53:291-299, 1972.

"Castration Anxiety and the Fear of Death," by I.
   Sarnoff J PERSONALITY   27:374-385, 1959.

"Death and Forever; Some Fears of War and Peace,"
   by S. Gifford ATLAN 209:88-92, March, 1962.

"Experimental and Correlational Studies of the
   Fear of Death," by D. Lester PSYCHOL BULL
   67:27-36, January, 1967.

"Fear of Death," NEWSWEEK 69:56, February 27, 1967.

"The Fear of Death," NM 125:152, November 10, 1967.

"Fear of Death," by E. J. Carnell CHRISTIAN CENT
   80:136-137, January 30, 1963.

"Fear of Death," by E. J. Carnell CHRISTIAN CENT
   80:367-368, March 20, 1963.

"Fear of Death," by E. Geiringer SPEC 189:179-180,
   August 8, 1952.

"Fear of Death: A Symptom with Changing Meanings,"by
   M. Eigen J HUMAN PSYCH 14:29-33, Summer, 1974.

"Fear of Death and Neurosis," by M. M. Stern AM
   PSYCH ASSN J 16:29-31, January, 1968.

"Fear of Death and Nightmare Exyeriences," by D.
   Lester PSYCHOL REP 25:437-438, October, 1969.

"The Fear of Death and the Fear of Dying," by L. J.
   Collett, et al. J PSYCHOL 72:179-181, July, 1969.

"Fear of Death and Trauma," by M. M. Stern INT J
   PSYCHOANAL 49:457-463, 1968.

"The Fear of Death as an Indispensable Factor in
   Psychotherapy," by H. R. Rosenthal AMER J
   PSYCHTHER 17:619-630, October, 1963.

"Fear of Death:Fear of Catastrophic Force," by
C. Marcus RNABC NEWS 9-10, August-September,
1972.

"Fear of Death in Parachute Jumpers," by M. Alexander, et al. PERCEPT MOT SKILLS 34:338, February, 1972.

"Fear of Death in the Mentally Ill," by H. Feifel,
et al. PSYCHOL REP 33:931-938, December, 1973.

"Fear of Death of Those in High Stress Occupations,"
by R. E. Ford, et al. PSYCHOL REP 29:502, October,
1971.

"The Fear of Death of Those Who Have Nightmares,"
by D. Lester J PSYCHOL 69:245-247, July, 1968.

"Fear of Dying and of Death as a Requirement of the
Maturation Process in Man," by G. Wittgenstein
HIPPOKRATES 31:765-769, November, 1960.

"Fear of Failure and Death," by R. J. Cohen, et al.
PSYCHOL REP 34:54, February, 1974.

"Helping Elderly Patients Face the Fear of Death,"
by K. Wolff HOSP COMM PSYCHIAT 18:142-144, May,
1967.

"How to Rise Above the Fear of Death," by N. V.
Peale, READ DIGEST 82:103-106, April, 1963.

"Inconsistency in the Fear of Death of Individuals,"
by D.Lester PSYCH REP 20:Suppl:1084, June, 1967.

"Management of Fear of Death in Chronic Disease,"
by J. Sheps J AM GERIAT SOC 5:793-797, 1957.

"Measurement of the Fear of Death: An Examination
of Some Existing Scales," by J. Durlak, J CLIN
PSYCHOL 28:545-547, October, 1972.

"The Need to Achieve and the Fear of Death," by D.
Lester PSYCHOL REP 27:516, October, 1970.

ATTITUDES TOWARD DEATH: FEAR OF DEATH

"Relationship Between Various Measures of Death
    Concern and Fear of Death," by J. Durlak
    J CONSULT CLIN PSYCHOL 41:162, August, 1973.

"School Phobia and the Fear of Death," by W.
    Tietz MENT HYG 54:565-568, October, 1970.

"Who's Afraid of Death ?" by H. Feifel, et al.
    J ABNORM PSYCHOL 81:282-288, June, 1973.

"Who's Afraid of Death on a Leukemia Ward? by
    J. Vernick, et al. AMER J DIS CHILD 109:393-397,
    May, 1965.

ATTITUDES TOWARD DEATH: FEAR OF THE DEAD
"Antecedents of the Fear of the Dead: An Analysis
    of Cultural Data," by D. Lester PSYCH REP 19:
    741-742, December, 1966.

"The Fear of the Dead in Nonliterate Societies,"
    by D. Lester J SOC PSYCHOL 77:283-284, April,
    1969.

"Necrophobia," by V. S. Pritchett NEW STATESM 69:
    684-685, April 30, 1965.

ATTITUDES TOWARD DEATH: GENERAL
"Anger Before Death," by E. K. Ross NURS 1:12-14,
    December, 1971.

"Appointment with Death. Attitudes and Communica-
    tions," by H. K. Silberman MO MED 70:37-42,
    January, 1973.

"An Approach to the Study of Death Attitudes," by
    R. A. Kalish AM BEHAV SC 6:68-70, 1963.

"Attempts to Ease Impact of Death in Contemporary
    Society Discussed at Rochester Conf Revd," THE
    NEW YORK TIMES 5:2 , May 9, 1971.

"Attitudes To Death," by J. V. Walker GERONT CLIN
    10:304-308, 1968.

"Attitudes Toward Attitudes Toward Death," by B.
    Crown, et al. PSYCHOL REP 20:Suppl:1181-1182,
    June, 1967.

"Attitudes Toward Death," by D. Cappon POSTGRAD
    MED 47:257, February, 1970.

"Attitudes Toward Death -- A Discussion," by R. L.
    Fulton J GERONT 16:63-65, 1961.

"Attitudes Toward Death and Bereavement," by C. J.
    Rosecrans ALA J MED SCI 8:242-249, April, 1971.

"Attitudes Toward Death, by P. Aries," (Review)
    by R. Boyers NEW REPUB 171:30-31, August 24, 1974.

"Attitudes Toward Death Discussed: International
    Gerontology Conference," THE NEW YORK TIMES
    13:2, August 13, 1960.

"Awareness of Fatal Illness," by K. Takashima, et
    al. JAP J NURS 35:29-43, October, 1971.

"Changing Attitudes to Death: A Survey of Contribu-
    tions in Psychological Abstracts Over a Thirty-
    Year Period," by M. Williams HUMAN RELATIONS
    19:405-423, November, 1966.

"Concept of Death," by F. Borkenau 20TH CENT 157:
    313-329, April, 1955.

"Concept of Pre-Death," by B. Isaacs, et al.
    LANCET 1:1115-1119, May 29, 1971.

"A Continuum of Subjectively Perceived Death,"
    by R. A. Kalish THE GERONT 6:73-76, 1966.

"Death and Attitudes Toward Death," (Symp.) GERIATRICS
    27:52+, August, 1972.

"Death, Ethics, and the National Board of Health and
    Welfare," by L. Leksell LAKARTIDNINGEN 70:3039-
    3040, September 5, 1973.

"Death Consciousness and Civilization," by J. T.
    Marcus SOCIAL RES 31:265-279, Autumn, 1964.

"Do We Need a New Death Concept?" LAKARTIDNINGEN
    63:2014-2015, May 25, 1966.

"Dr. G. Biorck of Serafin Hospital, Stockholm, Reveals Analysis of 84 Swedish Men and Women that Indicates 2/3 of Men and 1/3 of Women Want to Die Suddenly or Unexpectedly," THE NEW YORK TIMES 6:1, October 31, 1973.

"Dr. L. R. Kass Says that as a Result of Young Generation Having Grown up Without Fear of Lethal Childhood Diseases. People Are Becoming Less Conditioned to Accepting Death as Natural and Merciful Way to Terminate Aging Process," by W. Sullivan THE NEW YORK TIMES 17:2, February, 1971.

"The Dying Patient," by Wahl CONSULTANT 1:10+, November, 1961.

"Effect of a Friend Dying Upon Attitudes Toward Death," by D. Lester, et al. J SOC PSYCHOL 83: 149-150, February, 1971.

"Friendly Ear for Dying Patients," by B. Kovach READ DIG 102:37, June, 1973.

"How Do You Want to Die? Answers to a Questionnaire and Their Implications for Medicine," by G. Biorck ARCH INTERN MED 132:605-606, October, 1973.

"How the Living Look at Dying," by Cappon RN 28:45+, February, 1965.

"I Promise You, It Will Be All Right; The Dilemma of a Friend's Dying," by J. Barthel LIFE 72:55+, March 17, 1972.

"Interdisciplinary Attempts to Make Death in Contemporary Society More Dignified and Easier," THE NEW YORK TIMES 1:1, May 3, 1971.

"Intimations of Mortality: An Appreciation of Death and Dying," by C. D. Aring ANN INTERN MED 69:137-152, July, 1968.

"Is Acceptance of Non-Being Possible?" by C. J. Rosecrans ALA J MED SCI 7:32-37, January, 1970.

ATTITUDES TOWARD DEATH: GENERAL

"Is It Right to Joke With a Dying Man?" by E. Gott-
heil, at al. PRISM 2:17+, December, 1974.

"Man Ashamed; Reflections on Love, Sex and Death,"
by E. Heller ENCOUNTER 42:23-30, February, 1974.

"Man in Search of Meaning," by E. Marcovitz DEL MED
J 44:38-43, February, 1972.

"Mistaken Attitudes Toward Death," by C. Lamont
J PHILOS 62:29-36, January 21, 1965.

"Neglected Variables in the Study of Death Attitudes,"
by B. Chasin SOC Q 12:107-113, Winter, 1971.

"New York Times Survey of Changing Attitudes Toward
Death," THE NEW YORK TIMES 1:6, July 21, 1974.

"On the Failure to Forgive or Be Forgiven," by E. M.
Pattison AM J OF PSYCHOTHERAP 19:(1), 106-115,
1965.

"Public Attitudes and the Diagnosis of Death," by
J. D. Arnold, et al. JAMA 206:1949-1954, November,
25, 1968.

"Reflections on One's Own Death as a Peak Experience,"
by M. Hammer MENT HYG 55:264-265, April, 1971.

"Studies in Death Attitudes," by D. Lester PSYCHOL
REP 30:440, April, 1972.

"Symposium on Death and Attitudes Toward Death,"
GERIATRICS 27:52-60, August, 1972.

"They Saw a Burial Approaching," by Ritchie DIST-
RICT NURS 13:155+, November, 1970.

ATTITUDES TOWARD DEATH: GERIATRICS

"Age, Personality, and Health Correlates of Death
Concerns in Normal Aged Individuals," by P. J.
Rhudick, et al.   J   GERONT 16:44-49, 1961.

"Attitudes of Older Persons Toward Death: A Preliminary
Study (Attitudes Toward Death in Older Persons: A
Symposium)," by F. C. Jeffers, et al. J GERONT 16,
1:53-55, January, 1961.

"Attitudes Toward Death Among the Aged," by W. M. Swenson MINN MED 42:399-402, April, 1959.

"A Continuum of Subjectively Perceived Death," by R. A.
Kalish GERONT 6:73-76, June, 1966.

"Death, Dying, and Denial in the Aged," by L. R. Kimsey,
et al. AM J PSYCHIAT 129:161-166, August, 1972.

"Fear in Elderly People," by P. Williamson AM GERIAT
SOC 1:739-742, 1953.

"Helping Elderly Patients Face Fear of Death," by K.
Wolff HOSP COMM PSYCHIAT 18:142-144, May, 1967.

"Loss: A Constant Theme in Group Work with the Aged,"
by Burnside HOSP COMM PSYCHIAT 21:173+, June, 1970.

"Morbid Conditions at Death in Old Men," by B. Lake
J CHRON DIS 21:761-779, April, 1969.

"Old People Fight Death Worry Through Religion," SCI
N L 68:182, September 17, 1955.

"Older Persons Look at Death," by H. Feifel GERIAT 11:
127-130, March, 1956.

"On Morbid Thanatogenesis in the Aged," by E. Craciun,
et al. RUMAN MED REV 3:16-17, July-September, 1959.

"Personality Type and Reaction Toward Aging and Death,"
by K. Wolff GERIAT 21:189-192, August, 1966.

"The Social Loss of Aged Dying Patients," by B. A. Glaser
GERONT 6:77-80, June, 1966.

"Thought and Fear of Death in Aged with Mental Disorders,"
by C. Abraham SCHWEIZ ARCH NEUROL PSYCHIAT 90: 362-
369, 1962.

"Anticipation of Futurity of Ethnicity and Age,"
by D. K. Reynolds, et al. J GERONT 29:224-131,
March, 1974.

"Attitudes of Older Persons Toward Death: A Preliminary Study," by E. C. Jeffers, etal. J
GERONT 16:53-56, January, 1961.

"Attitudes Toward Death in an Aged Population," by
W. Swenson, et al. J GERONT 16:49--2, January,
1961.

"Attitudes Toward Death Among a Group of Acute
Geriatric Psychiatric Patients, " by A. E.
Christ J GERONT 16:56-59, january, 1961.

"Attitudes Toward Old Age and Death," by S. D. Shrut
MENT HEALTH 42:259-266, 1958.

"Consciousness of Death Across the Life Span," by
P. Cameron, et al. J GERONT 28:92-95, January,
1973.

"Decision-Making in the Death Process of the Ill
Aged," by M. B. Miller GERIATRICS 26:105-116, May,
1971.

"How Aged in Nursing Homes View Dying and Death,"
J. L. Roberts, et al. GERIATRICS 25:115-119, April,
1970.

"Maturation of Concepts of Death," by A. Maurer
BRIT J   MED AND PSYCH 39:35-41, 1966.

"Mental Life of Dying Geriatric Patients," by R.
Kastenbaum GERONT 7:97-100, June, 1967.

"Older Persons Look at Death," by H. Feifel GERIATRICS
11:127-130, March, 1956.

ATTITUDES TOWARD DEATH: GIVING UP
  "Dr. Richter Says Humans Can Die From Hopelessness,"
  THE NEW YORK TIMES 77:1, May 8, 1955.

ATTITUDES TOWARD DEATH: GIVING UP

"Is Death a Matter of Indifference?" by I. E.
   Alexander J   PSYCHOL 43:277-278, 1957.

"A Life Setting Conducive to Illness: The Giving up
   -- Given up Complex," by G. L. Engel ANN
   INT MED 69:293-300, 1968.

"Problems of Impending Death: The Concerns of the
   Dying Patient," by A. W. Reed J OF AM PHYSIC
   THERAP ASSN 48:740-742, 1968.

"Results of Questionnaire Concerning How People
   Want to Die Analyzed," by Biorck ARCH INTERN MED
   132:605-606, October, 1973.

"Thanatopsis in Hospitalized Patients," by M.
   Bialowas WIAD LEK 27:395-396, February 15, 1964.

ATTITUDES TOWARD DEATH: INDIVIDUALS
   "Difficult Patients: Laura Was Unpleasant and Made
   Us Angry. But She Was dying. And that Made Us
   Ashamed," by P. Reilly NURS '73 3:44-46, August,
   1973.

"Relationship Between Individual Attitudes Toward
   Life and Death, " by J. A. Durlak J CONSULT CLIN
   PSYCHOL 38:463, June, 1972.

"Vinnie Was Dying. But He Wasn't the Problem. I
   Was.," by E. B. Marino NURS '74 4:46-47, February,
   1974.

ATTITUDES TOWARD DEATH: MEASUREMENT
   "Death Concern: Measurement and Correlates," by L.
   S. Dickstein PSYCHOL REP 30:563-571, April,1972.

"Studies on Death-Attitude Scales," by D. Lester
   PSYCHOL REP 24:182, February, 1969.

ATTITUDES TOWARD DEATH: MENTALLY ILL PEOPLE
   "Attitudes of Mentally Ill Patients Toward Death,"
   by H. Feifel, et al. J NERV & MENT DIS 122:375-
   380, October, 1955.

"Attitudes of Schizophrenics with Respect to Life and Death," by H. Rotondo REV NEURO PSYCHIAT 16: 324-332, September, 1953.

"Attitudes Toward Death: An Emerging Mental Health Problem," by R. Fulton, et al. NURS FORUM 3:104-112, 1964.

"Attitudes Toward Death: A Psychological Perspective," by H. Feifel J CONSULT CLIN PSYCHOL 33:292-295, June, 1969.

"Attitudes Toward Death in Nightmare Subjects," by M. J. Feldman, et al. J ABNORM PSYCH 72:421-425, October, 1967.

"Attitudes Toward Death in Schizophrenia," by I. M. Greenberg J HILLSIDE HOSP 13:104-113, April, 1964.

"Attitudes Toward Death of Psychiatric Patients," by I. Halder INT J NEUROPSYCHIAT 3:10-14, February, 1967.

"The Day the President Was Assassinated: Patients' Reaction in One Mental Hospital," by R. V. Heckel MENT HOSP 15:48, January, 1964.

"The Death of a President: Reactions of Psychoanalytic Patients," by D. Kirschner BEHAV SCI 10:1-6, January, 1965.

"The Influence of Death Upon Hero-Identification Among Psychiatric Patients," by W. R. Bartz J SOC PSYCHOL 76:249-251, December, 1968.

"Mental Distress in the Dying," by Saunders NT 55: 1067+, October 30, 1959.

"Misgivings and Misconceptions in the Psychiatric Care of Terminal Patients," A. D. Weisman PSYCHIAT 33:(1) 67-81, 1970.

"Personality Reactions to the Diagnosis of Cancer," A. S. Norris J IOWA MED SOC 57:344-349, April, 1967.

"Possibility for Psychological Growth in a Dying Person," by J. C. Zinker, et al. GEN PSYCHOL 74: 197-199, April, 1966.

"The Psychological Care of Patients with Terminal Illness," by W. A. Cramond J R COLL GEN PRACT 22: 661-666, October, 1972.

"Psychological Reactions in Fatal Illness: the Prospect of Impending Death," by A. Verwoerdt, et al. J AM GERIAT SOC 15:9-19, January, 1967.

"Psychological Reactions to Impending Death," by J. L. Elmore, et al. HOSP TOP 45:35+, November, 1967.

"Schizophrenia and Death Concern," by D. Lester, et al. J PROJECT TECHN 33:403-405, October, 1969.

"A Study of Some Psychological Reactions During Prepubescence to the Idea of Death," by F. S. Caprio PSYCHIAT Q 24:495-505, 1950.

ATTITUDES TOWARD DEATH: NURSES
"Attitudes of Registered Nurses Toward Death in a General Hospital," by L. R. Shusterman, et al. PSYCHIAT MED 4:411-426, Fall, 1973.

"Attitude of Nursing Personnel Toward the Dying Patient," by M. Kivela SATRAANHOIJA 50:2-5, July 9, 1974.

"Attitudes to Death-bed Nursing," by R. Lamerton NURS TIMES 68:1544-1545, December 7, 1972.

"Attitudes to the Dying," by Turner NM 120:98, April 23, 1965.

"Attitudes Toward Death. A Comparison of Nursing Students and Graduate Nurses," by S. Golub, et al. NURS RES 20:503-508, November - December, 1971.

"Caring for the Chronic Sick and Dying. A Study of
Attitudes," by R. A. Strank NURS TIMES 68:166-169,
February 10, 1972.

"Dying Patients Still Have Human Needs," by G. W.
Downey MOD HOSP 114:78-81, March, 1970.

"Letter to a Nurse About Death and Dying," by E.
Kubler-Ross, NURS '73, 3:11-13, October, 1973.

"Nursing and Death. Death and Attitude Toward
Death," by H. Kono JAP J NURS 37:238-244,
February, 1973.

"Psychological Aspects of Nursing the Advanced Cancer Patient," by Sr. F. Xavier. NURS CLIN N AMER
2:649-658, December, 1967.

"The Social Ecology of Dying: Observations of Wards
for the Terminally Ill," by D. K. Reynolds, et al.
COMM PSYCHIAT 25:147-152, March, 1974.

"We Have No Dying Patients," by L. Robinson NURS
OUTLOOK 22:651-653, October, 1974.

ATTITUDES TOWARD DEATH: NURSING AIDES
"Attitudes Toward Death Among Nursing Home Personnel,"
by J. Pearlman, et al. J GENET PSYCHOL 114:63-75,
March, 1969.

"Effect of Work Experience in a Nursing Home on
the Attitudes Toward Death Held by Nurse Aides,"
by E. Howard GERONT 14:54-56, February, 1974.

"Psychological Aspects of Nursing the Advanced Cancer patieqt," by S. F. Xavier. NURS CLIN N AMER
2:649-658, December, 1967.

"The Social Ecology of Dying: Observations of Wards
for the Terminally Ill," by D. K. Reynolds, et al.
COMM PSYCHIAT 25:147-152, March, 1974.

"Attitudes of Nursing Students and Nursing Faculty Toward Death," by D. Lester, et al. NURS RES 20:50-53, January - February, 1974.

"Attitudes of Nursing Students Toward the Dying Patient," by R. C. Yeaworth, et al. NURS RES 23:20-24, January - February, 1974.

"Attitudes Toward Death. A Comparison of Nursing Students and Graduate Nurses," by S. Golub, et al. NURS RES 20:503-508, November-December, 1971.

"Changes in Nursing Students' Attitudes Toward Death and Dying. A Measurement of Curriculum Integration Effectiveness," by M. Snyder, et al. INT J SOC PSYCHIAT 19:294-298, Autumn, 1973.

"Nursing Students Learn to Face Death," by M. M. Folck, et al. NURS OUTLOOK 7, 9:510-513, September, 1959.

ATTITUDES TOWARD DEATH: OLD AGE
SEE ATTITUDES TOWARD DEATH: GERIATRICS

ATTITUDES TOWARD DEATH: OTHER CULTURES
"Anticipation of Futurity as a Function of Ethnicity and Age," by D. K. Reynolds, et al. J GERONT 29: 224-231, March, 1974.

"Attitudes Toward Death and Dying Among the Aymara Indians of Bolivia," by R. W. Tichauer J AMER ED WOM ASS 19·463-466, June, 1964.

"Cultural Factors in Loneliness, Death and Separation," by J. Yamamoto MED TIMES 98:177-183, July, 1970.

"Cultural Values and Attitudes Toward Death," by A. Howard, et al. J OF EXISTENT 6:161-174, 1965-1966.

"Death and Dreams and the Mexican-American," by C. Offir PSYCHOL TODAY 8:33+, October, 1974.

"Death in Africa, " by H. Collomb REV NEUROPSYCHIATR INFANT 18:827-836, October- November, 1970.

"Death in an Arab Culture," by J. Racy ANN NY ACAD
SCI 164:871-880, December 19, 1969.

"Death in the Hut of the Poor," by G. L. Townsend
J HIST MED 19:418, October, 1964.

"Death in the Primitive World. On the Question of
Death Suggestion in Melanesia," by G. Hofer
CONFIN PSYCHIAT 9:93-114, 1966.

"The Kuna Indians: Their Attitudes Toward the Aged,"
by R. L. Wolk, et al. J AM GERIAT SOC 19:406-416,
May, 1971.

"Medicine in Articulo Mortis in Nazi Prisons and
Concentration Camps," by R. Niewiarowicz PRZEGL
LEK 30:179-188, 1973.

"Mourning in Japan," by J. Yamamoto AM J PSYCHIAT
125:1660-1665, June, 1969.

"On the Significance of a Broken Home in Ethiopia,"
by R. Giel, et al. BRIT J PSYCHIAT 114:957-961,
August, 1968.

"Patterns of Morbidity and Mortality in Mexico
City," by D. J. Fox GEOG R 62:151-185, April, 1972.

"Repeated Hallucinatory Experiences as a Part of the
Mourning Process Among Hopi Women," by W. F.
Matechett PSYCHIATRY 35:185-194, May, 1972.

"Terminal Care at Home in Two Cultures," by J.
French, et al. AM J NURS 73:502-505, March, 1973.

"Young Collector Travels South of the Border:
Death Objects in Mexico," by D. St. Clair HOBBIES
62:25, September, 1957.

ATTITUDES TOWARD DEATH: PHYSICIANS
"Attitudes of and Towards the Dying," by D. Cappon
CAN MED ASS J 87:693-700, September 29, 1962.

"Attitudes of Medical Residents Toward the Dying
Patient in a General Hospital," by T. Rich, et al.
POSTGRAD MED 40:A127-130, October, 1966.

ATTITUDES TOWARD DEATH: PHYSICIANS

"Attitude Survey of Iowa Physicians," by Noyes,
et al. ARCH INTERN MED 132:607-611, October, 1973.

"Physicians' Attitudes Surveyed," by Goodnight MED
TRIB 15:1+, August 7,

"Physicians' Attitudes Toward the Dying Patient,"
by A. Pappert CAN DOCTOR 38:66+, October, 1972.

"Psychiatrist and the Dying Hospital Patient," by
F. F. Wagner MENT HYG 51:486-488, October, 1967.

ATTITUDES TOWARD DEATH: REACTIONS
"Reactions of a Man to Natural Death," by L. J.
Saul PSYCHOANAL Q 28:383-386, July, 1959.

"Reactions to an Approaching Death," by A. M.
Meisel, et al. DIS NERV SYST 26:15-24, January,
1965.

ATTITUDES TOWARD DEATH: RELIGION
"The Chaplain and the Dying Patient," by J. R.
Cavanagh HOSP PROG 52:34-40, November, 1971.

"Effect of Induced Fear of Death on Belief in Afterlife," by M. Osarchuk, et al. J PERS SOC PSYCHOL
27:256-260, August, 1973.

"Religiosity, Generalized Anxiety, and Apprehension
Concerning Death," by R. L. Williams, et al. J
SOC PSYCHOL 75:111-117, June, 1968.

"Religious Behavior and Concern About Death," by D.
Martin, et al. J SOC PSYCHOL 65:317-323, 1965.

ATTITUDES TOWARD DEATH: SENSE OF DYING
"Assessing the Views of the Dying," by J. Hinton
SOC SCI MED 5:37-43, February, 1971.

"Death and Dying: How Do You Really Feel About It?"
NURS '74 4:58-63, November, 1974.

"Death Concern, Futurity and Anticipation," by L.
S. Dickstein, et al. J OF CONSULT PSYCHOL 30:11-
17, 1966.

"Games People Play When They're Dying," by C. W.
Wahl MED ECON 46:106+, January 20, 1969.

"A Patient's Concern with Death," by Baker, et al.
AJN 63:90+, July, 1963.

"The Perception of Death," by Folta, NR 14:232+.
Summer, 1965.

"The Perception of Mortality," by J. Needleman ANN
NY ACAD SCI 164:733-738, December 19, 1969.

"Problems of Impending Death. The Concerns of the
Dying Patient," by Reed, PHYS THERAPY 48:740+,
July, 1968.

"The Sense of Being Dead and of Dying: Some Perspectives," by I. Fast, et al. J PROJECT TECHN 34:190-
193, June, 1970.

"The Sense of Dying," by J. A. Ryle GUY'S HOSP
REPORTS 99:223-235, 1950.

"What is Dying Like?" by M. A. Simpson NURS TIMES
69:405-406, March 29, 1973.

"What Is It Like to Be Dying?" by E. K. Ross JAP J
NURS   18:130-136, April, 1972.

ATTITUDES TOWARD DEATH: SEX DIFFERENCES
"Fantasies of Women Confronting Death," by E. Greenberger J CONSULT PSYCHOL 29:252-260, June, 1965.

"Flirting with Death: Fantasies of a Critically Ill
Woman, by E. Greenberger J OF PROJ TECH & PERSONAL
ASSESS 30:197-204, 1966.

"Noble Ladies (State of Mind at the Approach of
Death," by W. R. Rodgers NEW STATESMAN
41:706, June 23, 1951.

"Sex Differences in Attitudes Toward Death: a Rep-
lication," by D. Lester PSYCHOL REP 28:754, June,
1971.

ATTITUDES TOWARD DEATH: TIME SENSE

"Pseudo-Orientation in Time and Anticipated Parental Death," by A. Yanovski AM J CLIN HYPN 14:156-166, January, 1972.

BEREAVEMENT: BIBLIOGRAPHY ON
"Death and Bereavement: A Bibliography," by R. A. Kalish J HUMAN REL 13:118-141, First Quarter, 1965.

"Mourning: A Critical Survey of the Literature," by L. D. Siggins INT J PSYCHOANAL 47:14-25, 1966.

"Mourning: A Critical Survey of the Literature," by L. D. Siggins INT J PSYCHIAT 3:418-432, May, 1967.

BEREAVEMENT: CHILDREN
"Death, Delinquency and the Mourning Process," by M. Shoor, et al. PSYCHIAT Q 37:540-548, 1963.

"Grief and Mourning in Infancy and Early Childhood," by J. Bowlby PSYCHOANALYT STUDY OF THE CHILD 15:9-52, 1960.

"The Possible Consequences of Early Parent Death," by J. Birtchnell BRIT J MED PSYCH   42:1-12, March, 1969.

"Some Psychiatric Sequelae of Childhood Bereavement," by J. Birtchnell BRIT J PSYCHIAT 116:346-7, March, 1970.

"Why Children Must Mourn," by R. H. Agree, et al. TEACH 90:10+, October, 1972.

BEREAVEMENT: COUNSELING
"Caring for the Bereaved," by R. Gibson NURS MIRROR 139:65-66, October 10, 1974.

"Columbia University Foundation of Thanatology Conference," THE NEW YORK TIMES 56:1 November 4, 1973.

"Counseling the Bereaved," by R. L. Katz CCAR YRBK 63:465-469, 1953.

"Bereavement -- A Public Health Challenge," by F. J. Covill CANAD J PUBLIC HEALTH 59:169-170, April, 1968.

"Bereavement and the Acceptance of Professional Service," by Gerber COMMUN MENT HEALTH J 5:487+, December, 1969.

"Bereavement and the Care of the Bereaved," by S. Stephens MIDWIFE HEALTH VISIT 8:89+, March, 1972.

"The Dual Role of the Comforter and Bereaved," by E. Wallace, et al. MENT HYG 53:327-332, July, 1969.

"Emergency After Death," by R. E. Caughill HOSP TOP 51:37+, June, 1973.

"Grief and Bereavement. An Unmet Medical Need," by M. J. Krant DEL MED J 45:282-290, October, 1973.

"Help Your Patients to Mourn Better," by J. R. Hodge MED TIMES 99:53-64, June, 1971.

"Initial Responses to Grief. The Physician's Problems & Opportunities," by R. E. Buxbaum TEX MED 70:94-98, February, 1974.

"A Study of Bereavement," by N. Autton NURS TIMES 58: 1551-1552, December 7, 1962.

"To Comfort All that Mourn," by N. Autton NURS TIMES 58:1516+, November 30, 1962.

"You Will Cope, of Course," by I. M. Burnside AM J NURS 71:2354-2357, December, 1971.

BEREAVEMENT: DENTIST
"Death, Grief, and the Dental Practitioner: Thanatology as Related to Dentistry," by A. H. Kutscher, et al. J AM DENT ASSOC 81:1373-1377, December, 1970.

BEREAVEMENT: FAMILY
"The Camden Bereavement Project," by J. Leared MIDWIFE HEALTH VISIT 19:15-16, January, 1974.

"Grief and Mourning," by M. Dunlop AUST NURSES J 1:
22-24, December, 1971.

"Grief Reaction," by Pentney DISTRICT NURS 5:226+,
January, 1963.

"Grief Reactions Among University Students," by A.
M. Collins, et al. NAT ASSN WOMEN DEANS & COUNS
J 36:178-183, Summer, 1973.

"How Is Mourning Possible?" by M. Wolfenstein
PSYCHOANALYT STUDY OF THE CHILD 21:93-123, 1966.

"How We Face Sorrow and Grief," by J. Brothers GOOD
H 172:32+, January, 1971.

"Introjection in Mourning," by E. Jacobson INT J
PSYCHIAT 3:433-435, May, 1967.

"Is Grief a Disease?" by G. Engle PSYCHOMAT MED 23:
18-22, 1961.

"Learning to Live with Death and Grieving," by B. B.
Thomas, et al. UNA NURS J 69:9-17, April, 1971.

"Living with Grief," by Wylie FAMILY HEALTH 2:38+,
March, 1970.

"Loss and Grief," by A. M. Robinson J PRACT NURS 21:
18-19+, May, 1971.

"Mourning -- Death -- Ego," by J. Gillibert REV FRANC
PSYCHOANAL 31:143-171, January-February 1967.

"The Nature of Grief," by C. M. Parks INT J PSYCHIAT
3:435-438, May, 1967.

"Observations on Mourning," by I. Yalom NEW PHYSICIAN
13:80-81, March, 1964.

"On Death and Grieving," by M. Rees RNABC 15, August-
September, 1972.

"Personal Grief," C. Kinnish AUST NURSES J 2:20, April,
1973.

BEREAVEMENT: FAMILY

"The Clinical Morbidity of the First Year of Bereavement: A Review," by P. J. Clayton COMPR PSYCHIA 14: 151-157, March-April, 1973.

"The Consequences of Conjugal Bereavement," by D. Maddison NURS TIMES 65:50-52, January, 1969.

"Dealing With the Grieving Family," by Kalish RN 26:80+, May, 1963.

"Operational Mourning and Its Role in Conjoint Family Therapy," by N. L. Paul COMMUN MENT HEALTH J 1: 339-345, 1965.

BEREAVEMENT: GENERAL

"Attitudes Toward Death and Bereavement," by C. J. Rosecrans ALA J MED SCI 8:242-249, April, 1971.

"Bereavement," CANAD MED ASS J 97:1296-1297, November 18, 1967.

"Bereavement," MIDWIFE HEALTH VISIT 8:83, March, 1972.

"Chronic Grief," by P. L. Jackson AM J NURS 74:1288-1291, July, 1974.

"Concepts of Death and Grieving," T. Cauton PHILIPP J NURS 40:48-61, June, 1971.

"Death and the Road Back," by A. Winter J MED SOC NEW JERSEY 66:670-674, December, 1969.

"Grief," by V. R. Gray NURS '74 4:25, January, 1974.

"Grief," by Pentney NURS TIMES 60:1496+, November 13, 1964.

"Good Grief," by Westberg PN 12:14-15, March, 1962.

"Good Grief," SCI AM 220:52, April, 1969.

"Grief and Dying," by M. C. Moran HOSP PROGR 55:76+, May, 1974.

"Grief and Grieving," by G. L. Engel AM J NURS 64:93-98, September, 1964.

BEREAVEMENT: GENERAL

"Please Omit Sympathy," by W. Lowen READ DIG 66:59-61, March, 1955.

"Process of Mourning," by J. Bowlby INT J OF PSYCHO-ANAL 42:317-340, 1961.

"'Seeking' and 'Finding' a Lost Object: Evidence from Recent Studies of the Reaction to Bereavement," by C. M. Parkes SOC SCI MED 4:187-201, August, 1970.

"A Study of Normal Bereavement," by P. Clayton, et al. AM J PSYCHIAT 125:168-178, August, 1968.

"Thoughts on Bereavement," by S. Russel NURS TIMES 61:285-286, February 2, 1965.

"When Faced with Grief," by M. Wylie READ DIG 97:103-105, November, 1970.

BEREAVEMENT: GERIATRICS

"Grief Reactions in Later Life," by K. Stern, et al. AM J OF PSYCHIAT 108:289-294, 1951.

"Grief Work in the Aged Patient," by Burnside NURS FORUM 8:416+, Number 4, 1969.

BEREAVEMENT: OTHER CULTURES

"Mourning in Japan," by J. Yamamoto, et al. AM J OF PSYCHIAT 125:1660-1665, June, 1969.

"Repeated Hallucinatory Experiences as a Part of the Mourning Process among Hopi Indian Women," by W. F. Matchett PSYCHIATRY 35:185-194, May, 1972.

"The Socio-Cultural Expressions and Implications of Death, Mourning, and Bereavement Arising out of the War Situation in Israel," by P. Palgi J ANN PSYCHIAT 11:301-329, December, 1973.

BEREAVEMENT: PARENTS

"Social Work and the Mourning Parent: The Case of the Ill Child," by A. T. McCollum, et al. SOC WORK 17:25-36, January, 1972.

"Theory of Sympathy as the Starting Point in Nursing Philosophy.2. Tragedy of a Young Mother," by T. Odan JAP J NURS 37:228-233, February, 1973.

BEREAVEMENT: PARENTS

"Dual Role of the Comforter and the Bereaved: Reactions of Medical Personnel to the Dying Child and His Parents," by E. Wallace, et al. MENT HYG 53: 327-332, July, 1969.

"A Psychoendocrine Study of Bereavement. I. 17 Hydroxycorticosteroid Excretion Rates of Parents Following Death of Their Children from Leukemia," by M. A. Hofer, et al. PSYCHOSOM MED 34:481-491, November-December, 1972.

BEREAVEMENT: PETS
"The Pet and the Child's Bereavement," by Levinson MENT HYG 51:197+, April, 1967.

BEREAVEMENT: PSYCHIATRIC ASPECTS
"Activation of Mourning and Growth by Psychoanalysis," by J. Fleming, et al. INT J PSYCHOANAL 44:419-431, October, 1963.

"Bereavement and Mental Illness. 1 A Clinical Study of the Grief of Bereaved Psychiatric Patients. 2. A Classification of Bereavement Reactions," by C. M. Parkes BRIT J MED PSYCHOL 38:1-26, March, 1965.

"Bereavement as a Psychiatric Emergency," by A. Munro NURS TIMES 66:841-843, July 2, 1970.

"The Loss Complex: A Contribution to the Etiology of Depression," by G. Rochlin J OF AM PSYCHOANAL ASS 7:299-316, 1959.

"The Relevance of Conjugal Bereavement for Preventive Psychiatry," by D. Maddison BRIT J MED PSYCHOL 41: 223-233, September, 1968.

"Recent Bereavement as a Cause of Mental Illness," by C. M. Parkes BRIT J PSYCHIAT 110:198-204, March, 1964.

"Two Kinds of Guilt -- Their Relations with Normal and Pathological Aspects of Mourning," by L. Grinbern INT J PSYCHOANAL 45:366-372, April-July, 1964.

"Typical Findings in Pathological Grief," by V. Volkan PSYCHIAT Q 44:231-250, 1970.

BEREAVEMENT: PSYCHIATRIC ASPECTS

"Mania and Mourning," by W. C. Scott INT J PSYCHOAN-
AL 45:373-379, April-July, 1964.

"The Psychiatric Aspects of Bereavement," by A.
Bowen PRACTITIONER 210:127-134, January, 1973.

"Psychoneurotic Status During the Year Following
Bereavement," by A. H. Crisp, et al. J PSYCHOSOM
RES 16:351-355, August, 1972.

BEREAVEMENT: SOCIAL ASPECTS
"Social Isolation and Bereavement," by F. G. Wilson
LANCET 2:1356-1357, December 26, 1970.

"Social Isolation and Bereavement," by F. G. Wilson
NURS TIMES 67:269-270, March 4, 1971.

BEREAVEMENT: TRANSPLANT PATIENTS
"The Role of Grief and Fear in the Death of Kidney
Transplant Patients," by R. M. Eisendrath AORN J
11:71-77, January, 1970.

BEREAVEMENT: UNIVERSITY STUDENTS
"Grief Reactions Among University Students," by A.
M. Collins, et al. NAT ASSN WOMEN DEANS & COUNSEL
J 36:178-183, Summer, 1973.

BEREAVEMENT: WIDOWS AND WIDOWERS
"Anticipatory Grief and Widowhood," by P. J. Clayton,
et al. BRIT J PSYCHIAT 122:47-51, January, 1973.

"The Bereavement of the Widowed," by P. J. Clayton,
et al. DIS NERV SYST 32:597-604, September, 1971.

"Components of the Reaction to Loss of a Lamb, Spouse
or Home," by C. M. Parkes J PSYCHOSOM RES 16:343-
349, August, 1972.

"The Depression of Widowhood," by P. J. Clayton, et
al. BRIT J PSYCHIAT 120:71-77, January, 1972.

"Factors Affecting the Outcome of Conjugal Bereavement," by D. Maddison, et al. BRIT J PSYCHIAT 113:
1057-1067, October, 1967.

"The First Year of Bereavement," by C. M. Parkes
PSYCHIAT 33:(4) 444-467, 1970.

"Health After Bereavement," by C. M. Parkes, et al.
PSYCHOSOM MED 34:449-461, September-October, 1972.

"Introduction to Widowhood. The Role of the Family
Physician," by G. D. Clouse OHIO MED J 62:1281-
1284, December, 1966.

"Mortality and Morbidity in the First Year of Widowhood," by P. J. Clayton ARCH GEN PSYCHIAT 30:747-
750, June, 1974.

"Organization Helps SA Widows," by E. J. Stone
AUSTRALAS NURSES J 2:2, August, 1973.

"Paradoxical Response to Death of Spouse. Three Case
Reports," by J. H. Friedman DIS NERV SYST 25:480-
483, August, 1964.

"Problems of a Physician's Widow," WISCONSIN MED J
67:50, January, 1968.

"Problems of a Physician's Widow," WISCONSIN MED J
70:13, January, 1971.

"Widows and Widowhood," STATIS BULL METROP LIFE INS
CO 47:3-6, May, 1966.

"The Widow as a Caregiver in a Program of Preventive
Intervention with Other Widows," by P. R. Silverman MENT HYG 54:540-547, October, 1970.

"The Widow-to-Widow Program. An Experiment in Preventive Intervention," by P. R. Silverman MENT HYG
53:333-337, July, 1969.

CANCER: ATTITUDES OF PATIENTS
"Anticipating Death from Cancer -- Physician and
Patient Attitudes," by R. R. Koenig MICH MED 68:
899-905, September, 1969.

"Death in a Cancer Ward," TIME 93:62+, June 20, 1969.

"I Have Cancer," by J. Harris NURS MIRROR 138:71-71,
May 31, 1974.

"Living with Cancer," by B. M. Stewart NURS FORUM 13:
52-58, 1974.

CANCER: ATTITUDES OF PATIENTS

"Sometime Soon . . . I Will Be Dead of Cancer," MED
   INSIGHT 5:22-25, May, 1973.

"Terminal Cancer Ward: Patients Build 'Self Care At-
   mosphere of Dignity," JAMA 208:1289, May 26, 1969.

"To a Cancer Patient . . . Every Day Is Precious,"
   AUSTRALAS NURSES J 2:14, September, 1972.

CANCER: ATTITUDES OF PHYSICIANS
"Anticipating Death From Cancer -- Physicians and
   Patient Attitudes," by R. R. Koenig MICH MED 68:
   899-905, September, 1969.

"The Physician, His Patient and Cancerous Disease:
   A Terminal Period," by E. Raimbault REV MED PSYCH-
   OSOM 14:291-303, Autumn, 1972.

"What Does the General Practitioner Want to Know
   About the Cancer Patient?" by K. C. Calman, et al.
   LANCET 2:770-771, September 28, 1974.

CANCER: AWARENESS OF
"Patient Delay in Seeking Cancer Diagnosis: Behavioral Aspects," by R, K. Goldsen J OF CHRON DIS 16:
   427, 1963.

"Psychomatic Aspects of Cancer," by L. L. LeShan, et
   al. PSYCHOSOM MED 23:258-262, 1961.

CANCER: CARE
SEE CARE: CANCER PATIENTS

CANCER: CHILDREN
"Cancer in Childhood," BRIT MED J 3:136-137, July,
   20, 1968.

CANCER: COUNSELING
"Cancer Counselors," TIME 100:52, August 14, 1972.

CANCER:GENERAL
"Cancer and the Dying Patient," by L. J. Hertzberg
   AM J PSYCHIAT 128:806-814, January, 1972.

"Cancer Dwells Here," by M. Z. Davis NURS FORUM 6:
   379-381, Number 4, 1967.

CANCER: GENERAL

"Cancer Dwells Here," by J. Thompson NURS FORUM 7:
7-9, Number 1, 1968.

"The Cancer Gestalt," by M. J. Brennan GERIATRICS 25:
96-101, October, 1970.

"Letter: Cancer and the Patient," by E. L. Lloyd
BRIT MED J 4:674, December 15, 1973.

"Terminal Cancer," by M. J. Pilling NZ NURS J 64:
25-26, August, 1971.

"The Terminal Cancer Patient," by P. Copen NURS
CARE 6:27-30, May, 1973.

CANCER: HOME CARE
SEE HOME CARE: CANCER PATIENTS

CANCER: PSYCHIATRIC ASPECTS
"Cancer Mortality Rate: Some Statistical Evidence of
the Effect of Psychological Factors," by L. LeShan
ARCH OF GEN PSYCHIAT 6:333-335, 1962.

"Denial and Depression in the Terminal Cancer Patient
-- a Clue for Management," by R. D. Abrams PSYCHIAT
Q 45:394-404, Number 3, 1971.

"Denial as a Factor in Patients with Heart Disease
and Cancer," by T. P. Hackett, et al. ANN NY ACAD
SCI 164:802-817, December 19, 1969.

"Drug Treatment of Cancer," by L. A. Price NURS TIMES
68:1412-1413, November 9, 1972.

"Emotional Reactions to Chronic Disease with Emphasis
on Patients Suffering from Cancer," by G. Tourney
NORTHWEST MED 68:938-943, October, 1969.

"Forewarnings of Illness: Predictions and Premonitions
in Cancer Patients," by J. R. Lion et al. AM J OF
PSYCHIAT 125:137-140, 1968.

"Humanistic Aspects of Psychopharmacological Care of
the Terminal Cancer Patient," by B. L. Danto MICH
MED 72:833-834, December, 1973.

"The Patient with Inoperable Cancer from the Psychiatric and Social Standpoints: A Study of 101 Cases," by B. Gerle, et al. CANCER 13:1206-1217, 1968.

"Psychological Factors in the Outcome of Human Cancer," K. Stavraky, et al. J OF PSYCHOSOM RES 12(4):251-259, 1968.

"The Psychology of Terminal Illness as Portrayed in Solzhenitsyn's The Cancer Ward," by H. S. Abraham ARCH INTERN MED 124:758-760, December, 1969.

"Psychosocial Aspects of Advanced Cancer," by E. C. Payne, Jr., et al. JAMA 210:1238-1242, November 17, 1969.

"Psychological Problems in Terminal Cancer Management," by A. Rothenberg CANCER 14:1063-1073, 1961.

"Psychophysiological Aspects of Cancer," by C. Bahnson, et al. ANN NY ACAD SCI 125:733-1055, 1966.

"Rather Than Scream: What's It Like to Have a Terminal Disease?" by F. Brainard TODAYS HEALTH 49: 32-37, June, 1971.

"Reactions of Cancer Patients on Being Told Their Diagnosis," by J. Aitken-Swan, et al. BRIT MED J 1:779-783, 1959.

"Relief of Mixed Anxiety Depression in Terminal Cancer Patients. Effect of Thioridazine," by B. Johnston NY STATE J MED 72:2315-2317, September 15, 1972.

CANCER: SOCIAL NEEDS
"The Patient with Inoperable Cancer from the Psychiatric and Social Standpoints:A Study of 101 Cases," by B. Gerle, et al. CANCER 13:1206-1217, 1960.

"Psychosocial Aspects of Advanced Cancer," by E. C. Payne, et al. JAMA 210:1238-1242, November 17, 1969.

CANCER: TELLING THE PATIENT
SEE ETHICS: TELLING THE PATIENT

CANCER: WOMEN

"Care of Women with Terminal Pelvic Cancer," by J. K. Russell, et al. BRIT MED J 1:1214, 1964.

"Problems of Length of Terminal Care and Disthanasia in Patients with female Genital Cancer," by E. Klauber CESK GYNEKOL 37:176-179, April, 1972.

CARE: ADMINISTRATION
"Administrator Helps Determine Quality of Dying," by J. R. Kramer MOD NURS HOME 24:49+, April, 1970.

CARE: CANCER PATIENTS
"Care in Terminal Cancer," LANCET 2:352, August 12, 1967.

"Creative Support of a Cancer Patient," by Rev. R. D. Erickson BULL AM PROT HOSP ASS 34:15-21, Number 2, 1970.

"Management of Patients with Terminal Cancer,I," by W. L. Lirette, et al. POSTGRAD MED 46:145-149, December, 1969.

"Management of Patients with Terminal Cancer,II," by W. L. Linette, et al. POSTGRAD MED 47:202-206, January, 1970.

"The Management of the Patient with Advanced Cancer," by P. J. Mozden CA 19:211-217, July-August, 1969.

"Nursing Care of Patients with Advanced Cancer," by Boeker, et al. PUB SVC NURS MAG 44:463-466, August, 1952.

"Nursing of Patients Dying of Cancer," by Saunders NURS TIMES 55:1091+, November 6, 1959.

"Prosthetic Management of Terminal Cancer Patients," by R. Cantor, et al. J PROSTH DENT 20:361-366, October, 1968.

"Psychological Aspects of Nursing the Advanced Cancer Patient," by Mangen NURS CLIN N AMER 2:649+, December-1967.

CARE: CANCER PATIENTS

"Psychological Implications of Nursing Patients Suffering from Cancer," by A. D. G. Borzoni NURS TIMES 63: 1315, September 29, 1967.

"Reflections on Cancer Nursing," by J. E. Fox AM J NURS 66:1317-1319, June, 1966

"Team Approach to the Patient with Cancer," by J. Shepardson AM J NURS 72:481-491, March, 1972.

"Terminal Cancer: A Patient Oriented Approach," by R. K. Oldham J TENN MED ASS 63:206-208, March, 1970.

"Terminal Care in Malignant Disease," by M. R. Alderson BRIT J PREV SOC MED 24:120-123, May, 1970.

"Terminal Care of a Patient Suffering from Carcinomatosis," by F. Richards NURS MIRROR 138:78-80, April 19, 1974.

"Terminal Care of Cancer Patients," by M. R. Alderson BRIT J PREV SOC MED 24:65, February, 1970.

"The Terminal Care of Patients with Lung Cancer," by R. G. Twycross POSTGRAD MED J 49:732-737, October, 1973.

CARE: CHILDREN
SEE CHILDREN

CARE: COMFORTING PATIENTS
"A Bliss Before Dying?" NEWSWEEK 83:63-64, May 6, 1974.

"Comfort for Your Dying Patient," RN 25:63+, October, 1962.

"Communication and Comfort for the Dying Patient," by Drummond NURS CLIN N AM 5:55+, March, 1970.

"Don't Let Them Go Home in the Dark," PENN MED 74:68, January, 1971.

"A Good Birth -- A Good Life -- Why Not a Good Death?" by N. L. Fox J PRACT NURS 24:19-20, October, 1974.

CARE: COMFORTING PATIENTS

"Helping Patients Die Well," by M. J. Krant NEW ENG
J MED 280:222, January 23, 1969.

"Peaceful Death -- Assistance in Terminal Cases," by
S. Kubo KANGO KYOSHITSU 17:22-25, February, 1973.

"Serenity for a Terminally Ill Patient," by M. L.
Knipe AM J NURS 66:2252-2254, October, 1966.

"Specific Care for the Dying Patient," by J. L. Mathis
MED INSIGHT 4:53-55+, October, 1972.

"A Study in Terminal Care," by T. Yelverton NURS TIMES
67:293-296, March 11, 1971.

"Therapy of the Terminally Ill Patient," by T. Kostrubala ILL MED J 124:545-547, December, 1963.

"Thoughtful Care for the Dying," by C. R. Kneisl AM
J NURS 68:550-553, March, 1968.

"Total Care of the Terminally Ill," DIST NURS 14:103-
104, August, 1971.

CARE: COMMUNICATION IN
"Awareness of Death and the Nurse's Composure," by
J. C. Quint NURS RES CONF 1:98-126, April, 1965.

"Awareness of Death and the Nurse's Composure," by
J. C. Quint NURS RES 15:49-55, Winter, 1966.

"Communication and Comfort for the Dying Patient," by
Drummond NURS CLIN N AM 5:55+, March, 1970.

"Critique of Awareness of Death and the Nurse's
Composure," by R. C. Leonard NURS RES CONF 1:127-
134, April, 1965.

"Dealing with the Dying Patient," by C. P. Pattison,
et al. J KANS MED SOC 72:354-360, August, 1971.

"Death and Nursing. Death and Practice of Nursing.
Open Channel of Communication Between the Nurse
and the Patient," by H. Kono JAP J NURS 37:1346-
53, October, 1973.

"Dying Must Be Told Truth, Hospital Staff Told,"
HOSP PROGRESS 54:25, January, 1973.

"Dying Patient: An Unspoken Dialogue," by S. E.
Adelman NEW PHYSIC 20:706-708, November, 1971.

"Heed the Silent Cry!," by M. Mitchell SUPERV NURSE
4:58+, March, 1973.

"Helpful Words When Your Patient is Dying," by
J. P. Clark MED ECON 47:197+, September 28, 1970.

"Immediacy in Language: Channel to Care of the
Dying Patient," by S. R. Rochester et al. J COMM
PSYCHOL 2:75-6, January, 1974.

"Invisible Masks Hide Our Emotions," by E. A. Reed
AORN J 20:381-382, September, 1974.

"Listening to Relieve the Fear of Death," by M. E.
Westhoff SUPERV NURS 3:80+, March, 1972.

"Listening to the Dying," by R. Lamerton NURS TIMES
69:16, January, 1973.

CARE: COUNTRIES -- SOVIET UNION
"On Medical Care of Terminal Cases in Moscow," by L.
B. Shapiro, et al. ZDRAVOOKHR ROSS FED 10:20-22,
July, 1966.

"On the Organization of Terminal Care," by V. P.
Doroshchuk SOVET ZDRAVOOKHR 25:44-46, 1966.

"Our Experience in the Treatment of Terminal Cases,"
by A. I. Vakhovskii KLIN KHIR 4:41-45, April, 1965.

"Work Experience of the Specialized Brigade of an
Emergency Medical Service Station," by R. A.
Volynskii, et al. SOVET ZDRAVOOKHR 27:18-20, 1968.

CARE: COUNTRIES -- SWEDEN

"Terminal Care in Goteborg," by B. Lindegard LAKART-
INDINGEN 69:2675-2678, May 24, 1972.

CARE: COUNTRIES -- UNITED STATES OF AMERICA
"The Care of Terminal Patients: A Statewide Survey,"
by R. Noyes, Jr. J IOWA MED SOC 63:527-530, November, 1973.

"Death in American Experience," SOC RES 39:367-567,
Autumn, 1972.

"Death in American Experience: Review," by W. Hamilton
NEW REPUB 169:30, November 24, 1973.

"Dying in the USA," by R. Elder INT J NURS STUD 10:
171-184, August, 1973.

"Dying in the USA," by R. Elder NURS DIG 2:2-11, May,
1974.

"Personal Commentary on the Care of the Dying on the
North American Continent," by P. A. Downie, NURS
MIRROR 139:68-70, October 10, 1974.

CARE: ENVIRONMENT
"The Dying Patient and His Environment," by P. F.
Lehnert UGESKR LAEGER 134:1925-1927, September 4,
1972.

CARE: FAMILY
SEE FAMILY: CARE

CARE: FEMALES
"Treatment of a Dying Female Patient," by J. Norton
PSYCHE 22:99-117, February, 1968.

CARE: FOLK-LORE
"Customs Concerning Terminal Care and Death -- Notes
on Nursing Folk-Lore," by T. Yoneyama JAP J NURS ART
17:64-71, February, 1971.

CARE: GENERAL
"Aid to the Dying," by C. Aunders T ZIEKENVERPL 22:379-
381, April 15, 1969.

"The Approach to Death," by M. H. Webb-Peploe CHRIST NURS 238:23-24, December, 1971.

"Art of the Good Deathbedside Manner," by R. C. Bates MED ECON 47:183+, March 16, 1970.

"Care at the Last," NURS TIMES 66:1153, September 10, 1970.

"Care During Terminal Illness," by K. W. Woolley J PAST CARE 26:118-122, June, 1972.

"Care for the Chronic Sick and Dying," by R. A. Strank NURS TIMES 68:166-167, February 1 , 1972.

"Care for the Dying," CAN MED ASS J 91:926, October 24, 1964.

"Care for the Dying," by B. G. Morton PHYSIOTHERAP 58:124-125, April, 1972.

"Caring for the Terminally Ill," by Saunders HOSP 32: 56+, January 16, 1958.

"Caring for the Terminally Ill," by N. A. Miller NURS MIRROR 128:16, April 18, 1969.

"Care of the Dying," BRIT MED J 1:5, January 6, 1973.

"Care of the Dying," LANCET 2:753-754, October 2, 1971.

"Care of the Dying," LANCET 1:424-425, February 20, 1965.

"Care of the Dying," by M. R. Alderson BRIT MED J 1: 170, January 20, 1973.

"Care of the Dying," by W. C. Alvarez JAMA 150:86-91, September 13, 1952.

"Care of the Dying," by E. Anderson SA NURS J 38:28, June, 1971.

"Care of the Dying," by J. G. Bellows CONTEMP SURG 2:11-12, June, 1973.

"Care of the Dying, by M. B. Bennett S AFR MED J 47: 1558-1560, September 1, 1973.

"Care of the Dying," by D. Garland NURS TIMES 64:355-358, March 15, 1968.

"Care of the Dying," by R. Lamerton NURS TIMES 68:1544-1545, December 7, 1972.

"Care of the Dying," by B. McNulty NURS TIMES 68:1505-1505, November 30, 1972.

"Care of the Dying," by G. W. Milton MED J AUST 2:177-182, July 22, 1972.

"Care of the Dying," by W. Moore BRIT MED J 1:353-354, February 10, 1973.

"Care of the Dying," by J. T. Pembleton LANCET 2:820, October 9, 1971.

"Care of the Dying," by S. Roch NURS TIMES 64: Suppl: 157-160, October 11, 1968.

"Care of the Dying," by C. M. Saunders GERONT CLIN 9: 385-392, 1967.

"Care of the Dying," by S. L. Smith LANCET 1:555, March 10, 1973.

"The Care of the Dying Patient," J FLA MED ASS 46:438-440, October, 1959.

"Care of the Dying Patient," by N. Schnaper MED TIMES 93:537-543, May, 1965.

"Care of the Fatally Ill," by M. T. Root N ENG J MED 276:1040, May 4, 1967.

"The Care of the Patient in Terminal Illness," by McGrath CAN NURS 57:566, June, 1961.

"Care of Patients with Fatal Illness. Introductory Remarks," by L. P. White ANN NY ACAD SCI 164:637, December 19, 1969.

"The Care of Our Dying and Deceased Patients," by M. L. Schroder-Etzdorf AGNES KARLL SCHWEST 21:60-61, February, 1967.

"The Care of Terminally Ill Patients," by R. J. Noyes, Jr. ARCH INTERN MED 132:607-611, October, 1973.

"Death Watch," by M. Penalver AM J NURS 73:1916, November, 1973.

"Do We Forsake the Patient When He Is Dying?" by P. Siltala SATRAANHOITAJA 50:6-8, July 9, 1974.

"Dying and Terminal Care," by M. L. Boelen T ZIEKEN-VERPL 22:908-910, October 1, 1969.

"A First Glance at Terminal Care," by W. R. Moore J R COLL GEN PRACT 21:387-392, July, 1971.

"Help for the Dying," YNG LAEG 12:26-28, February 17, 1966.

"Help for the Dying," by Pastor AGNES KARLL SCHWEST 21:59-60, February, 1967.

"Help for the Dying Patient," by W. C. Alvarez GERIAT 19:69-71, February, 1964.

"Helping Patients Die," by E. E. Rinear PENN NURSE 29:2-8, March, 1974.

"Helping Patients Who Are Facing Death," by R. E. Kavanaugh NURS '74 4:35-42, May, 1974.

"Helping the Patient Prepare for Death," by R. Kastenbaum GERIAT 22:80+, February, 1967.

"Helping the Terminal Patient," HEALTH SOC SERV J 83:2950, December 15, 1973.

"How Can We Help the Dying?" by Green CONSULT 7:46+, June, 1967.

"How to Help the Patient Who Is Dying," by D. Raft AM FAM PHYS 7:112-115, April, 1973.

CARE: GENERAL

"Living Until Death," by R. G. Carey HOSP PROG 55:82-
87, February, 1974.

"Partners in Dying," by H. L. Muslin, et al. AM J
PSYCHIAT 131:308-310, March, 1974.

"Symposium: Care of the Dying. Approach to Death,"
by T. S. West NURS MIRROR 139:56-59, October 10,
1974.

"Symposium Care of the Dying. A Personal Commentary
on the Care of the Dying on the North American Continent," by P. A. Downie NURS MIRROR 139:68-70, October 10, 1974.

"Terminal Care," by J. M. Holford NURS TIMES 69: 113-
115, January 25, 1973.

"Terminal Care," by D. Kyle J R COLL GEN PRACT 21:382-
386, July, 1971.

"Terminal Care," by T. Kielanowski POL TYG LEK 27:81-
83, January 17, 1972.

"Thoughts on the Care of the Hopelessly Ill," by L. A.
Kohn MED TIMES 89:1177-1181, November, 1961.

"To Give Care in Terminal Illness," by R. P. Davidson, AM J NURS 66:74-75, January, 1966.

CARE: GERIATRICS
"Approach to the Dying Patient," by Green GERIAT NURS
2:16+, May-June, 1966.

"The Care of Dying Older Persons," by C. D. Leake
GERIAT 22:91-92, September, 1967.

"Care of the Dying in Geriatric Departments," by J.
Agate LANCET 1:364-366, February 17, 1973.

"Delivering Care to Older Dying Patients," by J. Carpenter, et al. PUB HEALTH REP 89:403-407, September-
October, 1974.

"Nursing Care of the Elderly: Human Problems of Nursing," NURS '73 3:18-22, April, 1973.

"When the Aged, Dying Patient Needs a Listener," by Birren RN 29:72+, December, 1966.

CARE: MANAGEMENT OF THE PATIENT

"The Care and Management of the Dying," by R. Noyes, Jr. ARCH INTERN MED 128:299-303, August, 1971.

"Errors in Management of Patients Dying of Chronic Obstructive Lung Disease," by C. C. Hunter, Jr. JAMA 199:488-491, February 13, 1967.

"Managing the Fatal Illness," by J. L. Bakke NORTHW MED 59:901-904, July, 1960.

"Management of Patients with Terminal Cancer," POST-GRAD MED 46:145-149, December, 1969.

"The Management of the Dying," by J. Roy J R COLL GEN PRACT 16:59-67, July, 1968.

"Management of the Dying Patient," CONN MED 33:78, February, 1969.

"The Management of the Dying Patient," by S. B. Khan SEMIN DRUG TREAT 3:37-44, Summer, 1973.

"The Management of the Dying Patient," by N. Schnaper MOD TREATM 6:746-759, July, 1969.

"Management of Terminal Illness," by R. P. Bergen JAMA 229:1352-1353, September 2, 1974.

"Management of the Patient with Terminal Illness," by J. E. Breed ILL MED J 139:503-505, May, 1971.

"Management of the Patient with Terminal Illness," by P. S. Rhoads JAMA 192:661-665, May 24, 1965.

"Management of the Terminally Ill Patient," by D. W. Bell VA MED MO 96:663-665, November, 1969.

CARE: NONACCOUNTABILITY

"The Nonaccountability of Terminal Care," by A. L. Strauss HOSP 38:73+, January 16, 1964.

CARE: NURSING -- IMPROVEMENT
"Improving Nursing Care of the Dying," by J. Quint NURS FORUM 6:368+, Number 4, 1967.

CARE: NURSING -- INTERACTION BETWEEN NURSE AND PATIENT
"Death and Dying: Anxieties, Needs and Responsibilities of the Nurse," by J. H. Barnsteiner J PRACT NURS 24: 28-30, June, 1974.

"Effect of Nurse-Patient Interaction on a Terminal Patient," by Olsen ANA CLIN SESS 90+, 1968.

"An Interaction Study Involving a Patient with a Guarded Prognosis," by L. McVay AM J NURS 66:1071-1073,1966

"Nursing and Death. Nurse's Role with the Patient Facing Death," by K. Ohara KANGO 24:1-7, September, 1972.

"Physician, the Nurse, and the Dying Patient," by F. P. Kosbab NEW PHYS 17:50-52, February, 1968.

CARE: NURSING SERVICES
"Acceptance of Death and the Nurse's Role," by A. Kokubu KANGO 24:8-13, September, 1972.

"Anxiety: Yours and Your Patient's," by N. S. Rickles, et al. NURS '73 3:23-26, March, 1973.

"Coping with a Job You Dread," by E. Kubler-Ross HOSP PHYS 9:30+. April, 1973.

"Death -- A Necessary Concern for Nurses," by M. J. Watson NURS OUTLK 16:47-48, February, 1968.

"Death and Bereavement -- The Nurse's Role," by J. Q. Benoliel AARN NEWS LETT 26:4-6, September-October, 1970.

"Death and Nursing. 8. Practice of Nursing of Terminal Cases, (1) Teamwork in Facing Death," by H. Kono JAP J NURS 37:1046-1052, August, 1973.

"Death and the Nurse," by C. M. Wallace NURS MIRROR 128:22, February 28, 1969.

"Death -- and the Nurse's Role," by L. M. Cordle RN 31:40-42, September, 1968.

"Death and the Role of Nursing," by S. Kubo KANGO KYO-SHITU 17:22-25, Autumn, 1973.

"Death in Nursing," by M. Teramoto KANGO 26:97-102, April, 1974.

"Discussion on Nursing Care to the Dying Patient,"by C. Tanaka, et al. JAP J NURS 36:714-727, June, 1972.

"Enough Time for Good Nursing," by V. Barckley NURS OUTLK 12:44-48, April, 1964.

"Improving Nursing Care of the Dying," by J. C. Quint, et al. NURS FORUM 6:368-378, Number 4, 1967.

"The Nurse and Death," by H. P. Wassermann S A NURS J 35:33-34, September, 1968.

"The Nurse and the Dying," by J. Bouchard BULL INFIRM CATH CAN 34:38-41, March-April, 1967.

"The Nurse and the Dying Patient," by K. Auvinen SATR-AANHOITAJA 48:736-738, September 25, 1972.

"The Nurse and the Dying Patient," by D. Maddison NURS TIMES 65:265-266, February 27, 1969.

"The Nurse and the Dying Patient," by D. Maddison T. ZIEKENVERPL 23:403-404, April 14, 1970.

"The Nurse -- Fellow-Being Confronted with Death, " by A. M. Elvings TIDSKR SVER SJUKSKOT 39:10-11, September 7, 1972.

"The Nurse in the Face of Death," by B. Dobbs Z KRAN-KENPFL 65:401-405, November, 1972.

"Nurses Accept Failure," by Kramer, et al. GERIAT NURS 3:8+, August, 1967.

"The Nurse's Contribution in Terminal Care," by B. J. McNulty NURS MIRROR 139:59-61, October 10. 1974.

"Nurses Discuss Death and Dying," AORN J 18:1262, December, 1973.

"Nursing Care for the Patient in Crisis," by R. Murray J PRACT NURS 23:20-23, April, 1973.

"Nursing Care of a Terminally Ill Patient," by M. Oda JAP J NURS 31:24-25, March, 1967.

"Nursing Care of the Dying," by H. R. Custer HOSP PROG 42:68, December, 1961.

"Nursing Care of the Dying and Terminally Ill Patient," KOREAN NURSE 11:59-73, December 25, 1972.

"A Nursing Care Study," by M. A. V. Lier NZ NURS J 67: 20-23, May, 1974.

"Nursing Service to Terminal Patients," REGAN REP NURS LAW 12:1, May, 1972.

"Nursing Services and the Care of Dying Patients: Some Speculations," by Quint NURS SCI 2:432+, December, 1964.

"Nursing Theory for Nurses. 10. Nursing and Dying Patients," by T. Kawakami, et al. JAP J NURS 36:1314-1318, October, 1972.

"Terminal Nursing Care," by J. P. Brown NURS TIMES 61: 1562, November 12, 1965.

"The Threat of Death: Some Consequences for Patients and Nurses," by J. C. Quint NURS FORUM 8:286-300, 1969.

"What Will Nursing Be Like in the '80's?" by H. Creight et al. MD NURSE 3:2, December, 1972.

CARE: NURSING SERVICES -- PROBLEMS
"Debating Terminal Care," by D. Lord HEALTH SOC SERV J 83:862, April 14, 1973.

"Difficult Patients Do Exist," by M. C. Parsons, et al. NURS CLIN N AMER 6:173-187, March, 1971.

"Dying Patient: A Difficult Nursing Problem," by J. C. Quint NURS CLIN N AMER 2:763-773, December, 1967.

"The Dying Patient: A Nursing Dilemma," by J. Q. Benoliel WASH J NURS 43:3-4, Janauary-February,1971.

"Excess Therapy in the Patient in the Terminal Phrase. I. Introduction," by P. H. Benavides GAC MED MEX 106: 95-96, August, 1973.

"Intercultural Problems in the Care of the Dying Patient," by G. S. Daynes AFR MED J 48:139-140, January 26, 1974.

"Obstacles to Helping the Dying," by J. C. Quint AM J NURS 66:1568-1571, July, 1966.

"Problem of the Dying Patient," NEW YORK J MED 65:2356-2366, September 15, 1965.

"Problems in the Care of the Dying," by J. M. Hinton J CHRON DIS 17:201-205, March, 1964.

"Problems of Impending Death. The Concerns of the Dying Patient," by A. W. Reed PHYS THERAP 48:740-743, July, 1968.

"Problems of Terminal Care in Lung Diseases," by R. Tybusz, et al. POL TYG LEK 26:1516-1518, September 27, 1971.

"Research into Problems of Terminal Care: Report from Westminster," NURS MIRROR 132:8-9, May 7, 1971.

"When Patients Die: Some Nursing Problems," by J. C. Quint CAN NURS 63:33-36, December, 1967.

CARE: NURSING SERVICES -- SPECIFIC EXPERIENCES
"Death and Me," by C. Krienke RN 32:51-53, September, 1969.

"Death Happened to My Patient," by W. S. Lin J NURS 15:78-79, July, 1968.

"Death of a Patient and Realization of One's Own Death -- Experience in Nursing a Dying Patient," by S. Mori COMPR NURS Q 5:47-54, Winter, 1970.

"Death of an Angel," by M. Bergner, et al. NURS '73 3:52-58, June, 1973.

"Death on a Ward," by Diaz HOSP TOP 47:83+, May, 1969.

"Death on a Ward," by T. Ingles NURS OUTLK 12:28, January, 1964.

"Don't Give up on Me!" by E. Hoffman AM J NURS 71:60-62, January, 1971.

"Experiences with Dying Patients," by J. J. Domning, et al. AM J NURS 73:1058-1064, June, 1973.

"First Death," by Dewey CATH NURSE 16:50+, September, 1967.

"I Was My Father's Nurse," by V. Chura AM J NURS 68: 1908-1909, September, 1968.

"My Dying Patient and Me," by S. Howard BEDSIDE NURS 4:17, November, 1971.

"My First Experience with a Dying Patient on the District," by Y. Mason QUEEN'S NURS J 17:131, September, 1974.

"My Nursing Experience. Death of Chinese Physician," by Y. Ishizuka JAP J NURS 34:86-89, July, 1970.

"My Unforgettable Nursing Experience. Heaven . . . It so Quickly Came. . .," by J. Decker J PRACT NURS 15:28, December, 1965.

"My Unforgettable Nursing Experience: Till Death Do Us Part," by Nuernberger PRACT NURS 14:27, December, 1964.

"The Nurse and Death," by H. P. Wassermann SA NURS J 35:24-25, October, 1968.

"Partners in Dying," by H. L. Muslin, et al. AM J PSYCHIAT 131:308-310, March, 1974.

"Shared Experience," by A. Bergman INT NURS REV 14: 39-42, September-October, 1967.

"Today I Saw Death," by S. Hingley AM J NURS 67:825, April, 1967.

CARE: NURSING STUDENTS

"An Experience. A 1st Year Student's First Confrontation with Death," by M. Welti Z KRANKENPFL 62:217-218, May, 1969.

"Grief and Dying:A Student Nurse's Experiences with a Terminal Patient," by M. C. Moran HOSP PROG 55: 76+, May, 1974.

"Life-Crisis Groups with Student Nurses. Massachusetts General Hospital," S AFR NURS J 33:20+, April, 1966; 33:27+, May, 1966.

"The Nurse's Most Difficult Function: Terminal Care," RN 27:45+, April, 1974.

"Nursing Students, Assignments, and Dying Patients," by J. C. Quint, et al. NURS OUTLK 12:24-27, January, 1964.

"Nursing Students Learn to Face Death," by M. Folck, et al. NURS OUTLK 7:510-513, September, 1959.

"A Student Looks at Death," by Roerig PRACT NURS 7: 14, March, 1957.

"A Student Nurse's Experiences with a Terminal Patient; Grief and Dying," by M. C. Moran HOSP PROG 55:76, May, 1974.

CARE: PAIN

"Care of the Dying. 6. The Pains of Death, " by R. Lamerton NURS TIMES 69:56-57, January 11, 1973.

"Death Often Is Not So Difficult or Painful," by W. C. Alvarez GERIAT 18:165-166, March, 1963.

CARE: PAIN

"Relief of Pain: Prerequisite to the Care and Comfort of the Dying," by E. Janzen NURS FORUM 13:48-51, 1974.

"Relieving Pain in the Terminally Ill," by M. M. Hurwitz GERIAT 28:56, May, 1973.

"Relieving Pain in the Terminally Ill," by M. Swerdlow GERIAT 28:100-103, July, 1973.

"The Role of Pain Relief in Terminal Care," by J. W. Lloyd NURS MIRROR 137:36-37, August 24, 1973.

CARE: PASTORAL

"Pastoral Care of the Dying," by N. Autton SPCK 127-136, 1966.

CARE: PHYSICAL

"Good Physical Care, Priority for the Dying," by R. P. Fleming RN 37:46-48+, April, 1974.

CARE: PHYSIOTHERAPY

"Physiotherapy and the Care of the Progressively Ill Patient," by P. A. Downie NURS TIMES 69:892-893, July 12, 1973; 922-923, July 19, 1973, 958-959, July 26, 1973.

CARE: PRIVACY

"Privacy for Dying Patients," NURS MIRROR 122:3, May 6, 1966.

CARE: PUBLIC HEALTH

"Customs Concerning Terminal Care and Death. Observation in Local Public Health Nursing Activities," by M. Shigamura, et al. JAP J NURS ART 17:72-76, February, 1971.

CARE: RECOVERY

"Death and Nursing. 5. The Concept of Recovery," by H. Kono JAP J NURS 37:634-638, May, 1973.

"11 Months of Nursing Without Giving up Hope," by S. Hasegawa KANGO 24:29-33, September, 1972.

"Our Experience in Retrieving Patients from Terminal States," by I. K. Gevorkian, et al. ZH EKSP KLIN MED 7:45-50, 1967.

CARE: RELIGION
   SEE RELIGION: CARE

CARE: TEAM APPROACH
   "Care of the Dying. 4. Teamwork," by R. Lamerton NURS
      TIMES 68:1642-1643, December 28, 1972.

   "Common Sense in the Intensive Care Unit," by H. A.
      Patterson BULL NY ACAD MED 47:1363-1364, November,
      1971.

   "The Incurable Patient and the After Care Unit," by
      H. Graber ORV HETIL 111:3053, December 20, 1970.

   "Needed: A New Approach to Care of the Dying," by
      Goetz RN 25:60+, October, 1962.

   "New Dimensions in Terminal Care," by P. Harris HOSP
      WORLD 1:12-13, October, 1972.

   "Organized Care of the Dying Patient," by M. J. Krant
      HOSP PRACT 7:101-108, January, 1972.

   "Terminal Care Units," by E. Wilkes J COLL GEN PRACT
      12:313-318, November, 1966.

CARE: TIME
   "Care of the Dying. 3. The Right Time to Die," R. Lam-
      erton NURS TIMES 68:1578, December 14, 1972.

   "Dying on Time. Arranging the Final Hours of Life in
      a Hospital," by Glaser, et al. HOSP TOPICS 43:28+,
      August, 1965.

   "The Last Hour Before Death," by M. Walker AM J NURS
      73:1592-1593, September, 1973.

CARE: TRANSPLANTS
   "By the London Post. Care of the Dying -- Kidneys for
      Transplant -- Topics of Common Concern," by J. Lis-
      ter N ENG J MED 289:679-681, September 27, 1973.

   "Life, Death, Kidney Transplantations and Nursing at
      the John Hopkins Hospital," by L. C. Parks ALUM MAG
      70:2-6, March, 1971.

"Care of the Dying," by I. Grant BRIT MED J 5060:1539-1540, December 28, 1957.

"The Care of the Dying," by F. Hebb CAN MED ASS J 65: 261-263, September, 1951.

"The Care of the Patient in Terminal Illness," by M. J. McGrath CAN NURS 57:566-571, June, 1961.

"The Care of the Patient with Cancer," by M. G. Patterson PUB HEAL NURS 42:377-385, July, 1950.

"Care of Patients with Fatal Illness," by L. P. White ANN NY ACAD SCI 164:637, December 19, 1969.

"Death and Dying: Anxieties, Needs and Responsibilities of the Nurse," by J. H. Barnsteiner J PRACT NURS 24: 28-30, June, 1974.

"Experimental and Correlational Studies of the Fear of Death," by D. Lester PSYCHOL BULL 67:27-36, January, 1967.

"Help for the Dying Patient," by W. C. Alvarez GERIAT 19,2:69-71, February, 1964.

"Help for the Hopeless," by C. Smith, et al. R I MED J 39,9:491-499, September, 1956.

"The Hopeless Case," by F. J. Ayd JAMA 181,13:1099-1102, 1962.

"The Management of Terminal Patients with Inoperable Carcinoma," by J. S. LaDue J KAN MED SOC 54,1:1-6, January, 1953.

"Managing the Fatal Illness," by J. L. Bakke NW MED 59, 7:901-904, July, 1960.

"The Nurse and the Dying Patient," by D. Maddison NURS TIMES 65:265-266, February 27, 1969.

"The Nurse and the Dying Patient," by C. M. Norris AM J NURS 55,10:1214-1217, October, 1955.

"The Nurse's Approach to the Patient Attempting to Adjust to Inoperable Cancer," by W. M. Kyle AM NURS ASS CONV CLIN SESS 27-39, 1964.

"Nursing Care of the Dying," by H. R. Custer HOSP PROG 42,12:68, 110-111, December, 1961.

"Nursing Services and the Care of Dying Patients: Some Speculations," by J. C. Quint NURS SCI 2:432-443, December, 1964.

"Nursing Students, Assignments, and Dying Patients," by J. C. Quint NURS OUTLK 12:24-27, June, 1964.

"On Those Who Care for the Sick," by J. Romano J CHRON DIS 1:695-697, 1955.

"The Physician, the Patient and Suffering," by P. Savery LAVAL MED 40:644-646, September, 1969.

"Professional Attitudes and Terminal Care," by C. Cameron PUB HEAL REP 67,10:955-959, October, 1952.

"Reflections on Cancer Nursing," by J. E. Fox AM J NURS 66:1317-1319, June, 1966.

"Serenity for a Terminally Ill Patient," by M. L. Knipe AM J NURS 66:2252-2254, October, 1966.

"Terminal Care," by W. F. Mengert ILL MED J 112,3:99-104, September, 1957.

"Terminal Care," by R. E. Tunbridge PRACT 196:110-113, January, 1966.

"Thoughtful Care for the Dying," by C. R. Kneisl AM J NURS 68,3:550-553, March, 1968.

"Thoughts on the Care of the Hopelessly Ill," by L. A. Kohn MED TIMES 89,11:1177-1181, November, 1961.

"Three Days with Mrs. M., " by C. Baxter AM J NURS 67, 4:774-778, April, 1967.

CARE: VISITORS

"Must It Be? Visitor Control in the Intensive Care Unit," by B. Martinson AM J NURS 70:1887, September, 1970.

CHILDREN: ANXIETY

"Anxieties of a Fatally Ill Boy," by I. M. Yakulis MATERN CHILD NURS J 2:121-128, Summer, 1973.

"Anxiety in the Dying Child," by J. J. Spinetta, et al. PEDIAT 52:841-845, December, 1973.

"Death Anxiety in Children with a Fatal Illness," by J. R. Morrissey AM J PSYCHOTHERAP 18:606-615, October, 1964.

CHILDREN: BEREAVEMENT

"Bereavement in Childhood," by B. Arthur, et al. J CHILD PSYCHOL PSYCHIAT 5:37-49, June, 1964.

"Bereavement in Children," by Davidson NURS TIMES 62: 1650+, December 16, 1966.

"Child Bereavement and Adult Psychiatric Disturbance," by O. W. Hill J PSYCHOSOM RES 16:357-360, August, 1972.

"Childhood Bereavement: Somatic and Behavioural Symptoms of Psychogenic Origin," by A. K. Geiger ARTS PAEDIATR ACAD SCI HUNG 14:159-164, 1973.

"Childhood Mourning and Its Implications for Psychiatry," by J. Bowlby AM J OF PSYCHIAT 118:481-498, December, 1961.

"Children's Experience with Death," by Zeligs MED INSIGHT 2:92+, March, 1970.

"Children's Reactions to Bereavement. Adult Confusions and Misperceptions," by S. I. Harrison ARCH GEN PSYCHIAT 17:593-597, November, 1967.

"Children's Reactions to the Death of Important Objects: A Developmental Approach," by H. Nagera PSYCHOANAL STUDY CHILD 25:360-400, 1970.

"The Impact of Object Loss on a Six Year Old," by M.
Chethik J AM ACAD CHILD PSYCHIAT 9:624-643, October,
1970.

"A Multigravida's Use of a Living Child in the Grief
and Mourning for a Lost Child," by P. Richardson
MATERN-CHILD NURS J 3:181-217, Fall, 1974.

"On Talking to Bereaved Burned Children," by T. S.
Morse J TRAUMA 11:894-895, October, 1971.

"The Pet and the Child's Bereavement," by B. M. Levinson MENT HYG 51:197-200, April, 1967.

"Psychiatric Sequelae of Childhood Bereavement," by
J. Birtchnell BRIT J PSYCHIAT 116:572-573, May, 1970.

"Some Psychiatric Sequelae of Childhood Bereavement,"
by A. Munro BRIT J PSYCHIAT 116:347-349, March, 1970.

"When Children Face Bereavement," by A. A. Lasker CON
JUD 18:53-58, 1964.

CHILDREN: BOOKS ABOUT DEATH
"S. R. Cole Article on Books for Children Based on
Theme of Death," THE NEW YORK TIMES 8:8, September
26, 1971.

"Young Children and Books on Death," by B. Morris EL
ENG 51:395-398, March, 1974.

CHILDREN: CARE
"Attitudes of Pediatricians Toward the Care of Fatally
Ill Children," by J. M. Wiener J PEDIAT 76:700-705,
May, 1970.

"A Basis for Nursing Care of the Terminally Ill Child
and His Family," by L. J. Hopkins MATERN-CHILD NURS
J 2:93-100, Summer, 1973.

"Can the Child Be Distracted from His Disease?" by N.
Issner J SCH HEALTH 43:468-471, September, 1973.

"Care of a Dying Child," by Y. Craig NURS MIRROR 137:
14-16, September 28, 1973.

"Care of the Child with a Fatal Illness," by R. W. Olmsted J PEDIAT 76:814, May, 1970.

"Care of the Child with Cancer," PEDIAT 40:487-546, September, 1967.

"Care of the Dying Child," by M. Green PEDIAT 40: Suppl:492-497, September, 1967.

"Care of the Young Patient Who Is Dying," by W. M. Easson   JAMA   205:203-207, July 22, 1968.

"The Chronically Ill Child Facing Death -- How Can the Pediatrician Help?" by R. K. Gould, et al. CLIN PEDIAT 12:447-449, July, 1973.

"Concept of Care for a Child with Leukemia," by J. Q. Benoliel NURS FORUM 11:194-204, Number 2, 1972.

"Death and the Pediatric House Officer," by J. E. Schowalter J PEDIAT 76:706-710, May, 1970.

"Dual Role of the Comforter and Bereaved: Reactions of Medical Personnel to the Dying Child and His Parents," by E. Wallace, et al. MENT HYG 53:327-332, July, 1969.

"Goal of Life Enhancement for a Fatally Ill Child: Rheumatoid Arthritis," by J. Morse CHILD 17:63-68, March, 1970.

"The Management of Fatal Illness in Childhood," by C. Saunders PROC ROY SOC MED 62:550-553, June, 1969.

"Our Experience in Therapy of Children in the Terminal Stage," by A. M. Verpakhovs'ka, et al. PEDIAT AKUSH GINEKOL 1:28, January-February, 1970.

"Our Ulleri Child: Death of a Child in a Little Asian Village," by P. Hitchcock REDBK 127:20+, August, 1966.

"The Pediatrician and the Handling of Terminal Illness," by R. S. Lourie PEDIAT 32:477-479, October, 1963.

CHILDREN: CARE

"Physician's Role in the Management of the Dying or Chronically Ill Child," by S. Lacey OH ST MED J 65: 259-260, March, 1969.

"Reactions to the Threatened Loss of A Child: a Vulnerable Child Syndrome. Pediatric Management of the Dying Child," by M. Green, et al. PEDIAT 34:58-66, July, 1964.

CHILDREN: CONCEPT OF DEATH
"Affective Responses to the Concept of Death in a Population of Children and Early Adolescents," by I. E. Alexander J GENET PSYCHOL 93:167-177, December, 1958.

"Chicago Psychoanalytic Institute -- 10 Year Study Indicates a Child's Reactions to Mourning May Be 'Exaggeration" of Adults; Holds True Mourning May Prevent Future Emotional Damage," NEW YORK TIMES 74:2, May 8, 1966.

"The Child's Concept of Death," by H. von Hug-Hellmuth PSYCHOANAL Q 34: 499-516, 1965.

"The Child's Perception of Death," by T. M. Miya NURS FORUM 11:214-220, 1972.

"Child's View of Death," by D. A. Vore S MED J 67: 383-385, April, 1974.

"The Child's Concept of Death," by E. Evelson REV PSI-COANAL 19:344-350, October-December, 1962.

"A Child's Preoccupation with Death," by N. A. Jackson ANA CLIN SESS 172-179, 1968.

"Children Ask About Death," by M. E. Lichtenwalner INT J RELIG ED 40:14-16, June, 1964.

"Children's Attitudes Toward Death," by R. Zeligs MENT HYG 51:393-396, July, 1967.

"Children's Awareness of Fatal Illness," by E. H. Waechter AM J NURS 7:1168-1172, June, 1971.

"Children's Awareness of Fatal Illness," by E. H. Waechter JAP J NURS 35:24-28, October, 1971.

"Children's Conceptions of Death," by J. D. Melear J GENET PSYCHOL 123:359-360, December, 1973.

"Children's Immediate Reactions to Death in the Family," by A. Yorukoglu TURK J PEDIATR 13:72-84, April, 1971.

"Cognizance of the Death Taboo in Counseling Children," by C. D. Berg SCH COUNSEL 21:28-33, September, 1973.

"The Concept of Death in Children," by W. Gartley, et al. J GENET PSYCHOL 110:71-85, March, 1967.

"The Concept of Death in Early Childhood," by P. Childers, et al. CHILD DEV 42:1299-1301, October, 1971.

"The Concept of Death in Midwestern Children and Youth," by M. S. McIntire, et al. AM J DIS CHILD 123:527-532, June, 1972.

"D. Barclay on Preparing Children to Comprehend Death," THE NEW YORK TIMES 6:28, July 15, 1962; LR:4, August 5, 1962.

"D. Barclay on Telling Children of Death in Family," THE NEW YORK TIMES 6:40:2, February 2, 1958.

"Death Fantasies in a Child," by J. Sichel PRAX KINDERPSYCHOL 16:172-175, July, 1967.

"The Distinction Between Living and Not Living Among 7-10 Year Old Children with Some Remarks Concerning the So-Called Animism Controversy," by G. Klingberg J OF GEN & PSYCH 105:227-238, 1957.

"Dr. E. Kubler-Ross Says Dying Children Can Often Deal Better with Impending Death than Parents," THE NEW YORK TIMES 43:2, January 23, 1972.

"Dr. L. Woodward Urges Parents Give Truthful Answers to Questions on Death," THE NEW YORK TIMES 22:1, June 8, 1954.

"Dr. M. S. Mahler Urges Teaching Children About Death to Lessen Their Anxiety if Close Relative Dies," THE NEW YORK TIMES 20:5, August 14, 1950.

"The Dying Child's Awareness of Death: A Review," by J. J. Spinetta PSYCHOL BULL 81:256-260, April, 1974.

"Helping Children to Accept Death," by M. S. Mahler CHILD STUDY 27, Number 4:98-99+, 1950.

"Helping Children to Mourn," by A. S. Watt MED INSIGHT 3:28-33+, July, 1971.

"Helping Your Child to Understand Death," by A. W. M. Wolf CHILD STUDY 35 Number 1:36-37, Winter, 1957-1958.

"How to Answer the Questions Children Ask About Death," by L. Chaloner PAR MAG 37, November, 1962.

"Interpreting Death to Children," by H. H. Sherrill, et al. INT J RELIG ED 28:4-6, October, 1951.

"The Meaning of Death to Children," by C. S. Adler AZ MED 26:266-276, March, 1969.

"Mommy, What Happens When I Die?" by P. G. Miller MENT HYG 57:20-22, Spring, 1973.

"Mommy, What Happens When I Die," by P. G. Miller, et al. NURS DIG 2:76-79, May, 1974.

"The Mourning Reaction of a Ten and a Half Year Old Boy," by Y. Gauthier PSYCHOANAL STUD CHILD 20:481-494, 1965.

"The Mourning Reaction of a Ten Year Old Boy," by Y. Gauthier CAN PSYCHIAT ASS J 11:Suppl:307-308, 1966.

"Observations Concerning Fear of Death in Fatally Ill Children and Their Mothers," by J. M. Natterson PSY-CHOSOM MED 22:456-465, November-December, 1960.

"Parents Group NYC Urges Discussion of Problem of Death with Children," THE NEW YORK TIMES 25:7, February 15, 1951.

"S. Ramos Article on How Parents Should Explain Death to Children," THE NEW YORK TIMES 6:94, December 10, 1972.

"Should Children Go to Funerals," by M. M. Kern PARENTS MAG 32:54+, February, 1957.

"A Study in Relationships Between the Life and Death Concepts in Children," by G. Safier J GENET PSYCH 105:283-294, December, 1964.

"What Death Means to Children," by H. Gibney PARENTS MAG 40, March, 1965.

CHILDREN: GENERAL
"A Child," NURS TIMES 63:991+, July 28, 1967.

"A Child Dies," by R. K. Chandra IN J PED 35:363-364, July, 1968.

"A Child Dies," by D. A. Howell SEM HEM 3:168-173, April, 1966.

"A Child Dies," by D. A. Howell HOSP TOP 45:93-96, February, 1967.

"The Child and Death," by M. Bellman LAKARTIDNINGEN 68:5555-5561, November 24, 1971.

"Child and Death," by T. B. Hagglund DUODECIM 89:1161-1167, 1973.

"Child and Death," by L. Michaux ACTA PAEDOPSYCHIATR 37:137-147, April-May, 1970.

"A Child Dies; A Nurse's Report," by J. E. Fretwell TIJDSCHR ZIEKENVERPL 27:36, January 8, 1974.

"Child in the Border-Line Situations of Life," by K. H. Schafer PRAXIS 61:1264-1267, October 10, 1972.

"Deaths in a Youth Program," by Faux, et al. MENT HYG 54:569+, October, 1970.

"The Dying Child," MED J AUST 1:1095-1096, May 22, 1971.

"The Dying Child," by M. V. Buhrmann S AFR MED J 47: 1114-1116, June 30, 1973.

"Dying Child," by F. C. Northrup AM J NURS 74:1066-1068, June, 1974.

"The Dying Child in the Hospital," by W. H. Wolters MAANDSCHR KINDERGENEESK 38:131-142, July, 1970.

"Dying -- Children and Adults," MED J AUST 1:1137-1142, May 22, 1971.

"The Dying and Death of the Child," by C. Bennholdt-Thomsen DEUTSCH MED WSCHR 84:1437-1442, August 14, 1959.

"Even a Dying Boy Can Teach Doctors Something," MED EC 51:246-247, February 4, 1974.

"Experience with Control of Terminal States in Children," by B. O. Nadraga, et al. PEDIAT AKUSH GINEK 2:29-31, March-April, 1967.

"How Well Prepared Are You for Death in the Young?" by Lescari PT CARE 4:91+, May 31, 1970.

"If a Child Must Die," by A. E. Evans NEW ENG J MED 278:138-142, January 18, 1968.

"Illness as a Crisis," by R. Murray J PRACT NURS 23: 22-25, March, 1973.

"Reflections on Incurably Sick Children," by P. Bigonesse LAVAL MED 40:651-654, September, 1969.

"The Repeatedly Ill Child: After You Diagnose Fatal Illness," by M. E. Prilook PAT CARE 7:36-37+, February 1, 1973.

"A Child witha Nasopharyngeal Sarcoma," by K. A. Mul-
elly NURS TIMES 67:348-351, March 25, 1971.

"Children and Death," by M. B. Clark VA MED MO 101:
573-576, July, 1974.

"A Child and Death," by K. Takeuchi JAP J NURS 37:194-
200, February, 1973.

"Children and Death," by S. Yudkin LANCET 1:37-41,
January 7, 1967.

"Children and Dying," by V. Taipale SAIRAANHOITAJA 48:
716-718, September 25, 1972.

"The Child, the Institution and Death," by C. Hordern
REV NEUROPSYCHIATR INFANT 21:203-215, April-May,
1973.

"Child with Leukemia," by C. E. Cragg CAN NURS 65:30-
34, October, 1969.

"Children Who Are Dying," by F. Smith TIJDSCHR ZIEKEN-
VERPL 26:603-608, June 5, 1973.

"Death in Childhood," CAN MED ASS J 98:967-969, May
18. 1968.

"The Death of a Child," by S. Fox NURS TIMES 68:1322-
1323, October 19, 1972.

"Death of a Child," by C. E. Koop BULL AM COLL SURG
52:173-174, July-August, 1967.

"Death on a Children's Ward," by E. N. Plank MED TIMES
92:638-644, July, 1964.

"Death on the Pediatric Ward," by E. Diaz HOSP TOP 47:
83+, May, 1969.

"Death Touched Our School," by F. H. Jacobi CHILD ED
43:85-86, October, 1966.

"Father Writes of His Child's Illness and Death," NURS TIMES 63:991-992, July, 28, 1967.

"Helping the Parents of Children with Leukemia," by V. Knapp, et al. SOC WORK 18:70-75, July, 1973.

"Interview the Parents of a Dead Child? Absolutely," by A. Freedman CLIN PEDIAT 8:564-565, October, 1969.

"Mothers' Perceptions of Care Given Their Dying Children," by D. Geis AM J NURS 65:105-107, February, 1965.

"Mourning Response of Parents to the Death of a Newborn Infant," by J. Kennell, et al. N ENG J MED 283:344-349, August 13, 1970.

"No Time for Fear," by Follett CAN NURS 66:39+, January, 1970.

"Observations Concerning Fear of Death in Fatally Ill Children and Their Mothers," by J. Natterson, et al. PSYCHOSOM MED 22:6:456-465, 1960.

"On a Teaching Hospital's Responsibility to Counsel Parents Concerning Their Child's Death," by H. Williams MED J AUST 2:643-645, October 19, 1963.

"Perinatal Death: The Grieving Mother," by P. Seitz, et al. AM J NURS 74:2028-2033, November, 1974.

"Resemblance of Parent-Child Death-Anxiety as a Function of Age and Sex of Child," by D. Lester, et al. PSYCHOL REP 31:750, December, 1972.

"The Seriously Ill or Dying Child:Supporting the Patient and the Family," by C. Koop PEDIAT CLIN N AM 16:555-564, August, 1969.

"Social Work and the Mourning Parent: The Case of the Ill Child," by A. McCollum, et al. SOC WORK 17:25-36, January, 1972.

"Tragedy of a Young Mother. 2 Guilt Complex of a Mother at the Death of Her Child," by T. Daidan JAP J NURS 37:342-347, March, 1973.

"The Attitude of Parents to the Approaching Death of Their Child," by J. Davis DEV MED CHILD NEUROL 6:286-288, June, 1964.

"Behavioral Observations on Parents Anticipating the Death of a Child," by S. Friedman, et al. PEDIAT 32: 610-625, October, 1963.

"Care of the Family of the Child with Cancer," by S. Friedman PEDIAT 40: Suppl:498-504, September, 1967.

"Childhood Leukemia: Meeting the Needs of Patient and Family," by J. Lukens, et al. MISS MED 67:236-241, April, 1970.

"Coping with a Child's Fatal Illness:A Parent's Dilemma," by S. Mann NURS CLIN N AMER 9:81-87, March, 1974.

"Dilemma of Trust:Relationship Between Medical Care Givers and Parents of Fatally Ill Children," by J. Kirkpatrick, et al. PEDIAT 54:169-175, August, 1974.

"Domestic Drips -- Pediatric Experiences with Parental Infusions in the Home," by S. Levin S AFR MED J 41:747-749, August 12, 1967.

"The Dying Child. Helping the Family Cope with Impending Death," by A. Smith, et al. CLIN PEDIAT 8:131-134, March 1969.

"Dying Child and His Family," by H. Branson BEDSIDE NURS 5:11-15, February, 1972.

"The Family and the Dying Child:A Compassionate Approach," by A. Lascari MED TIMES 97:207-215, May, 1969.

"Family Mediation of Stress:Childhood Leukemia," by D. Kapain, et al. SOC WORK 18:60-69, July, 1973.

"The Family of the Dying Child," by W. Easson, et al. PEDIAT CLIN N AM 19:1157-1165, November, 1972.

"The Family of the Fatally Burned Child," by H. Martin, et al. LANCET 2:628-629, September 14, 1963.

"Children and Death," by S. Yudkin LANCET 1:37-41, January 7, 1967.

"Death on a Children's Ward," by E. N. Plank MED TIMES 92,7:638-644, July, 1964.

"Dying and the Death of the Child," by C. Bennholdt-Thomsen DEUTSCH MED WSCHR 84:1437-1442, August 14, 1959.

"The Dying Child," by A. J. Solint DEV MED CHILD NEUROL 7:693-695, December, 1965.

"Experience with Control of Terminal States in Children," by B. O. Nadraga, et al. PEDIAT AKUSH GINEKOL 2:29-31, March-April, 1967.

"The Heart of a Child," by W. J. Potts JAMA 161, 6:487-490, June 9, 1956.

"How Well Prepared Are You for Death in the Young?" by Lescari PT CARE 4:91+, May 31, 1970.

"If a Child Must Die," by A. E. Evans NEW ENG J MED 278:138-142, January 18, 1968.

"Illness as a Crisis: The Terminally Ill Child," by R. Murray J PRACT NURS 23:22-25, March, 1973.

"Letter: More on the Value of a Personal relationship with the Fatally Ill Child," by R. Adler J PEDIATR 85:442-443, September, 1974.

"Management of the Child with a Fatal Disease," by R. Toch CLIN PEDIAT 3,7:418-427, July, 1964.

"Matter of Life and Death," by H. Galen YOUNG CHILD 27:351-356, August, 1972.

"Milieu Design for Adolescents," by J. Vernick, et al. AM J NURS 67:3, March, 1967.

"A Mother's Son," by A. Backers IMPRINT 19:17, December, 1972.

"The Multiple Meanings of the Loss of a Child," by C. E. Orbach AM J PSYCHOTHERAP 13:906-915, October, 1959.

"On Replacing a Child," by A. C. Cain, et al. J AM ACAD CHILD PSYCHIAT 3:443-456, July, 1964.

"Our Child Walks in the Valley of the Shadow," PARENTS MAG 27:38-39+, September, 1952.

"Reflections on Incurably Sick Children," by P. Bigonesse LAVAL MED 40:651-654, September, 1969.

"The Repeatedly Ill Child: After You Diagnose Fatal Illness," by M. E. Prilook PAT CARE 7:36-37+, February 1, 1973.

"The Repercussions of the Death of a Child," by D. McCarthy PROC ROY SOC MED 62:553-554, June, 1969.

"Response to a Dying Child," by D. A. Pacyna NURS CLIN N AMER 5:421-430, September, 1970.

"Shall This Child Die?" NEWSWEEK 82:70, November 12, 1973

"Something Can Be Done for a Child with Cancer," by M. Green, et al. HOSP TRIB 1, 27:8, July 3, 1967.

"Theme of Death in Children with Chronic Disease," by G. Raimbault, et al. ARCH FRANC PEDIAT 26:1041-1053, 1969.

"We Knew Our Child Was Dying," by J. Guimond AM J NURS 74:248-249, February, 1974.

"When a Child Is Dying," EMERG MED 6:182+, January, 1974.

"When Death Strikes the Child," NURS UPDATE 2:1+, August, 1971.

"Working with the Parent of a Dying Child," by L. Goldfogel AM J NURS 70:1674-1679, August, 1970.

CHILDREN: MEANING OF DEATH TO
"Child Animism: What the Child Means by 'Alive'," by S. W Klingensmith CHILD DEV 24,1:51-61, March, 1953.

CHILDREN: MEANING OF DEATH TO

"Children's Adaptation to Fatal Illness," by J. R. Morrissey J SOC WORK 8,4:81-88, October, 1963.

"The Distinction Between Living and Not Living Among 7-10 Year Old Children, with Some Remarks Concerning the So-Called Animism Controversy," by G. Klingberg J GENET PSYCHOL 90:227-238, 1957.

"A Note on Interviews with Children Facing Imminent Death," by J. R. Morrissey SOC CASEWORK 44,6:343-345, June, 1963.

"To Be Young and Know That Death Is Near: L. Helton's Osteogenic Sarcoman," by J. P. Blank READ DIG 100:78-84, June, 1972.

"What Death Means to Children," by H. H. Gibney PARENTS MAG 65:136-142, March, 1965.

CHILDREN: NURSES AND
"Nurse and the Terminally Ill Child," by F. Bright, et al. NURS OUTLOOK 15:39-42, September, 1967.

"A Nurse Looks at Children's Questions About Death," by D. J. Fredlund ANA CLIN SESS 105-112, 1970.

"Nursing Children with Cancer," by K. O. Preston NURS TIMES 67:467-469, April 22, 1971.

"Role of the Nurse in a Children's Cancer Clinic," by A. Tonyan PEDIAT 40,3:532-534, September, 1967.

CHILDREN: PSYCHIATRY AND
"Analysis of Behavior in a Terminally Ill Child," by B. Newcomer MATERN-CHILD NURS J 2:157-164, Fall, 1973.

"An Approach to the Emotional Support of Fatally Ill Children," by M. Karon, et al. CLIN PEDIAT 7,5:274-280, May, 1968.

"Childhood Mourning and Its Implications for Psychiatry," by J. Bowlby AM J OF PSYCHIAT 118:481-498, December, 1961.

"Death -- Its Psychological Significance in the Lives
of Children," by M. V. Buhrmann S AFR MED J 44:586-
589, May 16, 1970.

"Death Casts its Shadow on a Child -- Notes From a Psy-
chologist's Record," by R. Zeligs J NURS 15:26-32,
July, 1968.

"Death Fantasies in a Child," by J. Sichel PRAX KINDER-
PSYCHOL 16:172-175, July, 1967.

"The Death of an Infant:A Psychiatric Study," by G. L.
Bibring NEW ENG J MED 283:370-371, August 13, 1970.

"Depressive and Psychotic States as Anniversaries to Sibling Death in Childhood," by J. R. Hilgard INT PSYCH-
IAT CLIN 6:197-211, 1969.

"The Dread of Abandonment:A Contribution to the Etiology
of the Loss Complex and Depression," by G. Rochlin
PSYCHOLANALTIC STUDY OF THE CHILD 16:451-470, 1961.

"Emotional Impact of Childhood Leukemia," by E. O. Burgert, Jr. MAYO CLIN PROC 47:273-277, April, 1972.

"Fantasy Productions of Children with a Progressively
Crippling and Fatal Illness," by R. S. McCully J GENET
PSYCHOL 102:203-216, June, 1963.

"Pathological Mourning and Childhood Mourning," by J.
Bowlby AM PSYCHOANAL ASS 11:500-541, July, 1963.

"The Physician, the Child, and Death. 2 The Anguish of
Death During Psychotherapy of Children," by M. Geber
REV MED PSYCHOSOM 10:419-423, October-December, 1968.

"The Psychiatry of Terminal Illness in Children," by R.
V. Howarth PROC ROY SOC MED 65:1039-1040, November, 1972.

"Psychologic Impact of Long Illness and Death of Child
on Family Circle," by B. Cobb J PEDIAT 49:746-751,
December, 1956.

"Psychological Aspects of Sudden Unexpected Death in In-
fants and Children. Review and Commentary," by A. B.
Bergman PEDIATR CLIN N AM 21:115-121, February, 1974.

"Psychological Follow-up of Families with Childhood Leukemia," by J. A. Stehbens, et al. J CLIN PSYCHOL 30:394-397, July, 1974.

CHILDREN: REACTION TO PARENT'S DEATH
"Children's Reactions to the Death of a Parent:A Review of the Psychoanalytic Literature," by J. B. Miller J AM PSYCHOANAL ASS 19:697-719, October, 1971.

"Death of an Adult -- and Its Impact Upon the Child," by M. A. Wessel CLIN PEDIATR 12:28-33, January, 1973.

"The Effect of Parental Death Upon Children," by R. S. Workman J NY STATE NURS ASS 3:17-21, October, 1972.

"Further Data on Childhood Parent-Loss in Psychiatric Normals," by A. Munro, et al. ACTA PSYCHIAT SCAND 44: 385-400, 1968.

"The Late Effects of Loss of Parents in Childhood," by M. J. Gay, et al. BRIT J PSYCHIAT 113:753-759, July, 1967.

"Parental Loss by Death in Childhood as an Etiological Factor among Schizophrenic and Alcoholic Patients Compared with a Non-Patient Community Sample," by J. R. Holgard J NERV MENT DIS 137:14-28, July, 1963.

"When Their Daddy Died," by J. S. Winsor INT J RELIG ED 33:9+, April, 1957.

CHILDREN: RECOVERY
"Children Who Didn't Die," W. Strubbe TIJDSHR ZIEKEN-VERPL 27:224-226, March 5, 1974.

"Children Who Didn't Die. The So-Called 'Vulnerable Child' Syndrome," by W. Strubbe, et al. NED TIJDSCHR GENEESKD 116:1782-1786, September 30, 1972.

CHILDREN: SIBLINGS
"Children's Disturbed Reactions to the Death of a Sibling," by A. C. Cain, et al. AM J ORTHOPSYCHIAT 34:741-752, July, 1964.

"Dr. Alice Ginnott's Views that Children Should Not Be Encouraged to Take Father's Role at Expense of Their Childhood," THE NEW YORK TIMES 34:1, January 17, 1974.

"Effects on Family of Death of a Child; Notes Stress on Other Children," THE NEW YORK TIMES 20:1, September 15, 1973.

"How Surviving Parents Handled Their Young Children's Adaptation to the Crisis of Loss," by D. Becker, et al. AM J ORTHOPSYCHIAT 37:753-757, July, 1967.

"Preschool Child's Response to Death of Infant Sibling," by D. Weston, et al. AM J DIS CHILD 106,6:564-567,1963.

"Preventive Therapy with Siblings of a Dying Child," by D. Feinberg J AM ACAD CHILD PSYCHIAT 9:644-668, October 1970.

"A Young Boy's Reaction to the Death of His Sister. A Report Based on Brief Psychotherapy," by B. Rosenblatt J AM ACAD CHILD PSYCHIAT 8:321-335, April, 1969.

CHILDREN: STUDENT'S REACTIONS TO DEATH OF
"Students' Reactions to Children's Death," by G. N. Bonine AM J NURS 67:1439-1440, July, 1967.

"Three Medical Students Confront Death on a Pediatric Ward. A Case Report," by J. A. Griffith, et al. J AM ACAD CHILD PSYCHIAT 13:72-77, Winter, 1974.

CHILDREN: TELLING THEM ABOUT DEATH
"Death: Ways to Help Children Get Prespective," by L. B. Ames INSTR 78:59+, January, 1969.

"Do the Children Have to Know? Problem of Death," by M. Rudolph WOMANS HOME C 78:98-99+, October, 1951.

"Experts' Views on When and What Parents Should Tell Children About Death," THE NEW YORK TIMES 9:2, November 25, 1963.

"Explaining Death to Children," by P. L. Levin THE NEW YORK TIMES 6:47, February 21, 1965; 1:21, April 18, 1965.

"How Much Truth Can a Child Take?" by N. V. Peale FAMILY
CIRC 31, April, 1967.

"How Shall We Tell the Children?" by C. Hardgrove, et
al. AM J NURS 74:448-450, March, 1974.

"Interpreting Death to Children," by H. H. Sherrill, et
al. INT J RELIG ED 28:4-6, October, 1951.

"A Problem in Interpersonal Relations. Telling the Truth
to Leukemic Children," NURS CLIN N AMER 1:167-169,
March, 1966.

"Talking with Children About Death," by G. P. Koocher
AM J ORTHOPSYCHIAT 44:404-411, April, 1974.

"Way of Dialogue on Death Between Parents and Children,"
by E. A. Grollman RELIG ED 69:198-206, March, 1974.

"What I Tell a Dying Child's Parents," by C. E. Koop
READ DIG 92:141-145, February, 1968.

"What Shall We Tell Our Children About Death?" by E.
Yates NAT PAR TEACH 46:22-24, February, 1952.

"What Should the Child Know of Death?" by J. M. Wiener
MED INSIGHT 5:25-28+, April, 1973.

"What to Tell a Child with Acute Leukemia," TIME 93:67,
March 14, 1969.

"What to Tell a Dying Child," MED WORLD NEWS 14:68-69,
December 14, 1973.

"What to Tell Your Child About a Death in the Family,"
by Weinsheimer TODAYS HEALTH 38:29+, February, 1960.

"When a Child Is Told of Death," by D. Barclay THE NEW
YORK TIMES MAG 40, February 2, 1958.

"When Children Ask About Death," by R. Formanek EL SCHL
J 75:92-97, November, 1974.

"Care of a Baby with a Bone Marrow Transplant," by M. L. Byers, et al. NURS CLIN N AM 7:809-816, December, 1972.

"Death and the Young Child (Some Preliminary Considerations," by R. A. Furman PSYCHOANAL STUD CHILD 19:321-333, 1964.

"Death of a Young Child," by P. M. Spaulding AM J NURS 72:1281, July, 1972.

"Farewell to My Newborn Son," by A. E. Hotchner SAT EVE POST 227:17+, December 11, 1954; Discussion, 227:4, January 15, 1955.

"Some Peculiarities of the Clinical Picture and Therapy of Terminal States of Pneumonia of Young Children," by A. M. Moldavskii PEDIATRIIA 46:68-70, August, 1967.

"Students' Reactions to Children's Deaths," by G. N. Bonine AJN 67:1439+, July, 1967.

"Sudden Death in the Crib," by Oshin RN 25:58-59, January, 1962.

"Thoughts on the Death of a Five-Day-Old Child," by M. Higgins GOOD H 139:26-27, August, 1954.

"When an Infant Dies Unexpectedly," by Ernsting PN 8:7+, September, 1958.

"Young Children and Death," by E. N. Plank YOUNG CHILD 23:331-336, September, 1968.

DEATH: DIGNITY IN
"Human Dignity, Healing Art and Care for the Dying," by L. Wallden LAKARTIDNINGEN 62:3113-3117, September 29, 1965.

"Let Your Patient Die With Dignity," by M. M. Ravitch MED TIMES 93:594-596, June, 1965.

DEATH: DISTRESS IN
ALSO SEE DRUGS
"Analgesia During the Terminal Stage of Disease," by F. F. Wagner CAH ANESTH 17:595-602, October, 1969.

"Analgesics in Terminal Disease," by C. Saunders, et al.
BR MED J 3:245, July 24, 1971.

"Are We Trying Too Hard?" by R. Kenyon NEBR STATE MED J
54:81-82, February, 1969.

"Buffering the Deadly Impact," JAMA 205:238, July 22,
1968.

"Can Death Ever Be Merciful? Pro and Con Discussion,"
by T. Gallagher, et al. GOOD H 174:90-91+, June, 1972.

"Conference Discusses New Research Findings on Care of
the Dying Patient," THE NEW YORK TIMES 1, May 3, 1971.

"Death Agony," by G. Leleu LILLE MED 11:1024-1027, November, 1966.

"Distress in Dying," BR MED J 5354:5400, August 17, 1963.

"Distress of Dying," by W. D. Rees AM HEART J 86:141-142,
July, 1973.

"The Distress of Dying," by W. D. Rees BR MED J 3:105-
107, July 8, 1972.

"The Distress of Dying," by W. D. Rees NURS TIMES 68:1479-
1480, November 23, 1972.

"Distress of Dying," by R. Lamerton BR MED J 3:351, August 5, 1972.

"Distress of Dying," by M. A. Simpson, et al. BR MED J
3:231, July 22, 1972.

"Distress of the Dying," LANCET 1:927-928, April 27,
1963.

"Dying: Medicine Can Fend Off Death, But in Doing So It
Often Merely Prolongs Agony," by R. S. Morison SCI AM
229:55+, September, 1973.

"Dying in Peace," by P. Mauriac PRESSE MED 61:1413,
October 31, 1953.

"Easy Death," by R. P. Brooks, Jr. TIME 76:58, October 24, 1960.

"Easiest Way to Die," by J. Steinbeck SAT R 41:12+, August 23, 1958; Reply. E. S. Seiler 41:26, September 6, 1958.

"Good and Bad Death," by L. Lattes MINERVA MED 1:842-854, April 4, 1953.

"Kindness of Strangers," by R. T. Millard GOOD H 166:56+, March, 1968.

"Medicine, Man and Suffering," by R. Champagne LAVAL MED 40:647-648, September, 1969.

"Must Medical Progress Leave the Dying Patient Behind?" by M. Kerstein GERIAT 28:67-68, April, 1973.

"The Needs of the Dying," by L. Wallace NURS TIMES 65:1450-1451, November 13, 1969.

"On Pain of Death," by D. Warr NZ NURS J 68:21-24, October , 1974.

"The Pains of Death," NURS TIMES 69:56-57, January 11, 1973.

"The Physical and Mental Distress of the Dying," by J. M. Hinton QUART J MED 32:1-21, January, 1963.

"The Preservation of Life," by N. K. Brown, et al. JAMA 211:76-82, January 5, 1970.

"The Problem of Pain in the Dying Patient," by B. McNult QUEENS NURS J 16:152+, October, 1973.

"Suffering and Death," by R. Champigny SYMPOSIUM 24:197-205, Fall, 1970.

"Tranquillity of Death," by J. D. Ratcliff READ DIG 56:124-126, February, 1950.

"Very Easy Death," Review by M. Muggeridge TIME 87:124+, May 20, 1966.

"Absurb Quest," by W. R. Mueller, et al. KENYON R. 29: 223-245, March, 1967.

"All That Live . . . " NT 66:1172, September 10, 1970.

"And the Cells Grow," by M. F. Knox AM J NURS 70:1047, May, 1970.

"Answer to the Article,'Theory and Therapy of Dying," by V. Spangenberg PSYCHIAT NEUROL 40:324-325, July 16, 1958.

"Anthropology and Death. Apropos of the Lyons Experience of the Institut of Legal Medicine," by J. P. Do, et al. MED LEG DOMM CORPOR 5:157-161, April-June, 1972.

"Approach to Death," by T. S. West NURS MIRROR 139:56-59, October 10, 1974.

"An Appropriate Death," by L. Feigenberg LAKARTIDNINGEN 68:5965-5975, December 15, 1971.

"Boundaries, by R. J. Lifton," Review by E. Capouya SAT R 54:28-29+, February 20, 1971.

"This Business of Dying," by H. M. Cronk NURS TIMES 68: 1100, August 31, 1972.

"The Business of Dying," by F. P. Hsii NURS J SINGAPORE 14:38-39, May, 1974.

"Checking on the Harlequin," by D. Lester PSYCHOL REP 19:984, December, 1966.

"Confrontation with Death," by L. M. Rombouts T ZIEKEN-VERPL 22:904-907, October 1, 1969.

"The Confrontation with Death," by E. deWind INT J PSY-CHOANAL 49:302-305, 1968.

"Confronting the Decision to Let Death Come," by N. H. Cassem CRIT CARE MED 2:113-117, May-June, 1974.

"Conquest of Death," by E. Geiringer SPEC 189:210, August 15, 1952. Discussion. 189:242,270,298,334,364+, August 22 -- September 19, 1952.

"Conscious of Death," SCI DIG 64:68, September, 1968.

"Coping with Untimely Death," by A. D. Weisman PSYCHIAT 36:366-378, November, 1973.

"Crisis: Death and Dying," by Agullera ANA CLINN SESS 269+, 1968.

"Dead on Arrival," by D. Sudnow TRANS-ACTION 5:36-43, 1967.

"Dealing with Dying," by V. R. Gray NURS '73 3:26-31, June, 1973.

"Death," NURS TIMES 58:1035, August 17, 1962.

"Death," NURS TIMES 63:1599, December 1, 1967.

"Death," T ZIEKENVERPL 22:376, April 15, 1969.

"Death," by M. Frost NURS MIRROR 132:41-42, January 29, 1971.

"Death," by P. Hopkins IMPRINT 20:20, December, 1973.

"Death and Dying," by R. F. Newcome RN 35:1, August, 197

"Death and Dying," by D. E. Sobel AM J NURS 74:98-99, January, 1974.

"Death and Dying," by A. L. Winner J R COLL PHYS LOND 4:351-355, July, 1970.

"Death and Life," by E. Torp SYKEPLEIEN 54:129, March 15, 1967.

"Death and Modern Man," TIME 84:92+, November 20, 1964.

"Death in Life," by A. Wenkart J EXIST 7:75-90, 1967.

"Death is Alone:Excerpt from Death and Hope," by H. J. Cargas CATH WORLD 210:269-272, March, 1970.

"Death is No Outsider," by C. Staff PSYCHOANALYSIS 2:56-70, 1953.

"Death of a Human Being," LANCET 2:590-591, September 11, 1971.

"Death of a Man," Review by P. Taylor SAT R 40:20, April 20, 1957.

"Death of Death? Concerning L. Boros' Mystery of Death," NEWSWEEK 67:53, January 24, 1966.

"Death of Human Beings," by J. Kobayashi KANGO 24:41-46, May, 1972.

"Death in the Suburbs," by J. A. Myers, Jr. ENG J 52: 377-379, May, 1963.

"Death of the Human Being," by J. Kobayashi INT NURS REV 20:62-63, March-April, 1973.

"Death Revisited," by J. Watson J AM VET MED ASS 165:73, August 15, 1974.

"Discussion:Man and Death," by H. Kawano, et al. JAP J NURS 38:155-172, February, 1974.

"The Dying," by D. Cappon PSYCHIAT Q 33:466-489, July, 1959.

"Dying," by E. S. Hjortland, et al. MINN MED 50:1761-1762, November, 1967.

"Dying," by R. S. Morison SCI AM 229:54-60+, September, 1973.

"Dying and Death," RESUSCIATION 1:85-90, July, 1972.

"Dying -- Out of Darkness," TIME 94:60, October 10, 1969.

"Dying vs. Well-Being," by R. Koenig NURS DIG 2:49-54, May, 1974.

"Empathy: From Broadway to Death's Door," by J. J. Gill MED INSIGHT 3:36-38, February, 1971.

"Evolution in the Graveyard," by H. Hahn MIDWEST Q 10: 275-290, April, 1969.

"Facing Death," by R. M. Cooper, et al. CHR CENT 90:225-232, February 21, 1973.

"The Fade-Out," by S. Vaisrub ARCH INTERN MED 121:571, June, 1968.

"The Final Care," by H. T. Dam, et al. T ZIEKENVERPL 23:400-402, April 14, 1970.

"Hope in the Midst of Horror," by R. L. Cleath CHR TODAY 14:3-5, March 27, 1970.

"The Hopeless Patients," by S. Hathirat J MED ASS THAI 55:543-547, September, 1972.

"How America Lives with Death," by K. L. Woodward NEWS-WEEK 75:81-82+, April 6, 1970.

"I Swear by Appolo the Healer," by A. D. Gunn NURS MIR-ROR 501-502, January 28, 1966.

"If Tragedy Comes," by Z. Popkin CORONET 33:61-64, March, 1953.

"Illness as a Crisis," by R. Murray J PRACT NURS 23:20-23, February, 1973.

"In the Face of Death," by M. Finnerty, et al. INFIRM CAN 13:27-30, August, 1971.

"Incurables," by S. Cohen J REHAB 33:16+, September - October, 1967.

"Journey's End," by H. Ogilvie PRACTITIONER 179:584-591, October-December, 1957.

"Last Enemy," CHR TODAY 18:31-34, March 29, 1974.

"The Last Night," by L. Andrews AM J NURS 74:1305-1306, July, 1974.

"Last Rights," by M. Mannes FAM HEALTH 6:24-25+, June, 1974.

"Last Rights, by M. Mannes," Review by M. Maddocks
TIME 103:83, January 7, 1974.

"Last Rights, by M. Mannes," Review by M. Muggeridge
ESQUIRE 81:52+, March, 1974.

"The Last Stages of Life," by C. Saunders AM J NURS
65:70-75, March, 1965.

"The Last Stages of Life," by C. Saunders IRISH NURS
NEWS 6-10, November-December, 1965.

"The Last Stages of Life," by C. Saunders T NORSK LAE-
GEFOREN 87:248-252, February 15, 1967.

"Let's Face It," by J. McDonell NZ NURS J 68:13-14, July,
1974.

"Letter from Leete's Island: A Case of Termination," by
J. Fischer HARPER 246, 24-27, February, 1973.

"Life and Death," by R. Amyot BULL INFIRM CATH CAN 36:
121-124, May-June, 1969.

"Life and Death," by Conley, et al. TOM NURS 4:20+, October - November, 1963.

"Life, Death and Creation," by M. Ledoux REV FR . PSYCH
36:585-598, July, 1972.

"Life or Death," by D. Wittner TODAY'S HEALTH 52:48-53,
March, 1974.

"Living Until Death," by R. G. Carey HOSP PROG 55:82-87,
February, 1974.

"Living and Dying," Review by G. Gunn NEW REPUB 171:28,
September 21, 1974.

"Logistics of Dying," by D. Sudnow ESQUIRE 68:102-103+,
August, 1967.

"Lonely Business," NEWSWEEK 57:56, May 22, 1961.

"The Loneliness of Death," by R. Ristau AJN 58,9:1283-1284, September, 1958.

"Man Facing a Threat to Life," by W. Rudolf MED KLIN 56:2013, November 24, 1961.

"Man Facing Death," by R. Burnand CONCOURS MED 81:4771-4773, November 7, 1959.

"A Matter of Spirit," by M. C. Tinsley NURS TIMES 64:1764, December 27, 1968.

"Message of the Kite," by D. R. Stewart READ DIG 95:122-125, July, 1969.

"Miracles Don't Happen," by Long RN 19:52+, March, 1956.

"The Moment of Death," NZ MED J 75:97-98, February, 1972

"The Moment of Death," by L. E. Rozovsky CAN HOSP 49:24-25, September, 1972.

"Moratorium Day," AJN 69:2645, December, 1969.

"Neither Life Nor Death," by L. M. Miller READ DIG 55-59, December, 1960.

"New Obscenity," by L. H. Newton COMMONWEAL 101:304-305, January 3, 1975.

"Normality, Mask of Death," by J. Chambon REV FR PSYCH 36:421-425, May, 1972.

"Observations on Death and Dying," by M. A. Lieberman GERONT 6:70-72, 1966.

"Observations on Life and Death," by S. Iihama JAP J NURS ART 12:87-89, April, 1966.

"Of Life's Span -- the Final Stages," by D. Wingquist NURS HOMES 22:32-34, March, 1973.

"On Death," by Drake TOM NURS 4:14+, August-September, 1963.

"On Death," by K. Friesner RESP CARE 19:536-538, July, 1974.

"On Death and Dying," by D. W. Berg, et al. J MED ED 47: 587-588, July, 1972.

"On Death and Dying," by L. Feigenberg LAKARTIDNINGEN 68:5811-5821, December 8, 1971.

"On Death and Dying," by E. Kubler-Ross, et al. JAMA 221:174-179, July 10, 1972.

"On Dying and Death," by R. Schweingruber Z KRANKENPFL 59:305-308, May, 1966.

"On Dying and Death," by J. T. Schwidde ROCKY MT MED J 70:23-26, November, 1973.

"On First Encountering Death," by D. Welch J PRACT NURS 24:32-33, March, 1974.

"On the Road to the River," by J. W. Reid CAN MED ASS 91:911-913, October 24, 1964.

"On the Road to the River," by J. W. Reid NS MED BULL 52:3-5, February, 1973.

"Patients in Limbo," by Davis AJN 66:746+, April, 1966.

"A Perfect End," NURS TIMES 67:577, May 13, 1971.

"Prescription for Dying," TIME 57:58-59, April 2, 1951.

"The Problem of Death," by G. A. Leng SING MED J 10:71, June, 1969.

"Review Essay: On Death and Dying," by G. Nettler SOC PROB 14:335-344, Winter, 1967.

"The Right Way of Dying," by G. J. Hardeman TIJDSCHR ZIEKENVERPL 26:1297-1298, December 18, 1973.

"The Running Down Toward Death," by R. Ehrenberg STUD GEN 559-566, December, 1951.

"Sentenced to Not to Be Allowed to Die," by B. Hook
LAKARTIDNINGEN 67:6102-6104, December 23, 1970.

"Shape of Death," TIME 77:51, January 20, 1961.

"Signs of Death," by M. Fishbein MED WORLD NEWS 12:80,
December 10, 1971.

"The Small Blue Notebook," NURS TIMES 69:1299-1300, October 4, 1973.

"Small Talk 50: On Death and Dying," by H. Schneider Z
ALLGEMEINMED 50:586-587, April 30, 1974.

"Some Aspects of Death," by W. C. Alvarez GERIAT 19:465-
466, July, 1964.

"Study on Dying," by W. Schweisheimer MED KLIN 67:268-
269, February 25, 1972.

"Terminal Illness," by E. C. Thomas DIST NURS 4:156+,
October, 1961.

"Terminal Patients and 'No Code' Orders," REGAN REP NURS
LAW 14:1, November, 1973.

"To Be or Not To Be -- Alive or Dead?" by J. W. Still J
AM GERIAT SOC 17:522-524, May, 1969.

"This Is One Boy's Message to You From Korea," AM MAG
156:6, August, 1953.

"Through the Valley of the Shadow," by B. Graham READ
DIG 98:107-110, April, 1971.

"To Die Alone," by Roose MENT HYG 53:321+, July, 1969.

"To Pass Through Death," CHR CENT 77:435, April 13, 1960.

"Until Death Ensues," by B. A. Davis NURS CLIN N AM 7:
303-309, June, 1972.

"Way of Dying," ATLAN 199:53-55, January, 1957.

DEATH: GENERAL

"We All Make Mistakes," NURS MIRROR 136:12, January 26,
1973.

"When Death Comes," NEWSWEEK 72:54, December 9, 1968.

"When the Curtain of Death Parted," by M. C. Sampson
READ DIG 74:48-51, May, 1959.

DEATH: HUMOR
"How to Exit Laughing," by K. Featherman CURR MED DIG
37:1040-1042, November, 1970.

"Humor and Death," by W. E. O'Connell PSYCHOL REP 22:
391-402, April, 1968.

DEATH: LANGUAGE OF
"Death in Our Language," by H. J. Lubbe SA NURS J 33:12-
13, May, 1966.

"Judgement Day: Quotations," by N. D. Fabricant TODAYS
HEALTH 34:29, March, 1956.

"Last Words of the Great," by W. Saroyan NATION 217:282,
September 24, 1973.

"Learning the Language of Death," by E. Kubler-Ross
HOSP WORLD 1:18+, June, 1972.

"Party of One: Deathbed Utterances," by C. Fadiman HOL-
IDAY 12:6+, November, 1952. Discussion. 13:4, January, 1953.

"Quotations on Dying," THE NEW YORK TIMES 6:80, March
21, 1965.

"Words That Didn't Die," by R. Clark MCCALLS 83:28+,
November, 1955.

DEATH: MEANING OF
"Acceptance of Death -- Beginning of Life," by J. B.
Graham N CAR MED J 24:317-319, August, 1963.

"The Aging Process and the Meaning of Death," by J. Q.
Benoliel IMPRINT 20:10-11, February, 1973.

"Another Journey; Reprint," READ DIG 78:167-168, May, 1961.

"Any Man's Death Diminishes Me," NEW ENG MED J 278: 1455, June 27, 1968.

"An Appreciation of Death and Dying," by C. Aring HOSP TRIB 6, June 26, 1967.

"As I Lay Dying," NEWSWEEK 48:77, September 17, 1956.

"Between Immortality and Death: Some Further Reflections on the Summa Contra Gentiles," by A. C. Pegis MONIST 58:1-15, January, 1974.

"Changing Concepts of Death," by J. J. Lowrey AORN J 15:91+, February, 1972.

"Changing Concepts of Death," by J. J. Lowrey HAWAII MED J 30:251-257, July-August, 1971.

"A Clinical Perspective on Dying," by R. G. Janes CAN MED ASS J 107:425-427, September 9, 1972.

"Comments About the Meaning of Life," by C. M. Norris KANS NURS 45:1-3, October, 1970.

"The Concept of Death," by I. Suig TIDSKR SVER SJUKSKOT 41:4-11, May 3, 1974.

"The Concept of Pre-Death," by B. Isaacs, et al. LANCET 1:1115-1118, May 29, 1971.

"The Confrontation with Death," by E. deWind INT J PSY-CHOANAL 49:302-305, 1968.

"Crisis: Moment of Truth," by D. C. Aguilera J PSYCHIAT NURS 9:23-25, May-June, 1971.

"Dealing with Death," NEW ENG J MED 289:539-541, September 6, 1973.

"Death -- A Natural Process," by J. B. Clemmons, Jr. BLACK BAG 2:20-21, March, 1973.

"Death: A Radicalization," by J. Carmody CHR CENT 91:
639-640, June 12, 1974; Discussion. 91:830, September
4, 1974.

"Death and My Life," by A. Beberman R METAPHYS 17:18-
32, September, 1963.

"Death As a Fact of Life," Review by L. C. Lewin NATION
216:538-540, April 23, 1973.

"Death As A Fact of Life; Excerpt," by D. Hendin SCI DIG
73:34-39, June, 1973.

"Death Be Not Distorted," by J. Zazzaro NATIONS SCH 91:39-
42+, May, 1973.

"Death Belongs to Life," by L. S. Vander Werf UND CHILD
21:51-52, April, 1952.

"Death? Don't Know," by R. Menahem REV INFIRM 24:211-
214, March, 1974.

"Death in the Nuclear Age," by H. J. Morgenthau COMMENT-
ARY 32:231-234, September, 1961.

"Death Isn't Necessary," by A. W. Galston SCI DIG 58:80-
85, July, 1965.

"Death: Process or Event?" by R. S. Morison SCIENCE 173:
694-698, August 20, 1971.

"The Distinction Between Life and Death," T SYGEPL 66:
423, October, 1966.

"Dying: A Meaningful Summation of Life," by M. Krant
MED INSIGHT 5:26-29, January, 1973.

"Dying Is Also Living," by M. Hoevet NURS CARE 7:12-15,
July, 1974.

"Dying -- Some Issues and Problems," by R. Pritchard
ANN NY ACAD SCI 164:707-719, December 19, 1969.

"Empty Slogan for the Dying," by F. J. Ingelfinger NEW
ENG J MED 291:845-846, October 17, 1974.

"Facing Death," by J. M. Hinton J PSYCHOSOM RES 10:22-
28, July, 1966.

"Facing Death," by Stevens NURS TIMES 58:777-778, June
15, 1962.

"Facing Death," E. deWind PSYCHE 22:423-441, June, 1968.

"Facing Up to Death: Terminally Ill Patients," by E. K.
Ross TODAYS ED 61:30-32, January, 1972.

"The Foreshortened Life Perspective," by R. Kastenbaum
GERIAT 24:126-133, August, 1969.

"Going Downhill-- A Lethal Journey," by J. Diamond J
KEN MED ASS 58:710-714, June, 1960.

"How Do You Stand?" by S. DeSales AORN J 6:40-43, October, 1967.

"I Don't Intend to Die This Year," by C. Safran TODAYS
HEALTH 50:24-30, September, 1972.

"Illness and Dying Seen As Status Changes," by D. M.
Platt AUST NURS J 67:92-96, May, 1969.

"The Imminency of Death," by P. Cameron J CONSULT CLIN
PSYCHOL 32:479-481, August, 1968.

"Intimations of Mortality. An Appreciation of Death
and Dying," by C. D. Aring ANN INTERN MED 69:137-152,
July, 1968.

"It Comes to Us All," by J. M. Mead NURS MIRROR 132:40,
January 29, 1971.

"Life Is a Terminal Illness," by R. Drake CHR CENT 89:
744-745, July 5, 1972.

"The Light That Brought Death Out of Darkness," by C.
Marcus RNABC NEWS 11-2, August-September, 1972.

"Matter of Death and Life; Life-Giving Death," CHR CENT 81:291, March 4, 1964.

"Maturation of Concepts of Death," by A. Maurer BRIT J MED PSYCHOL 39:35-41, March, 1966.

"Meaning of Death," SAFETY ED 40:12-13, March, 1961.

"Meaning of Death," TIME 75:52+, January 11, 1960.

"Meaning of Death," by W. Cloud POP SCI 182:21-22, September, 1963.

"Meaning of My Own Death," by A. Paskow INT PHILOS Q 14: 51-69, March, 1974.

"More Thoughts About Dying," by Wilmshurst NURS TIMES 55:441+, April 10, 1959.

"Must It Be?" by B. Martinson AM J NURS 70:1887, September, 1970.

"Myth-Conceptions About Death," by Vernon and Payne J RELIG HEALTH 12:63-76, January, 1973.

"No Groveling Death!" by E. Hoagland NEWSWEEK 82:8-9, July 30, 1973.

"The Obligation to Live vs. the Option to Die," by S. M. Simons S MED J 65:731, June, 1972.

"On Dealing with the Realities of Death,' by A. Pappert CAN DOCTOR 38:66-69, September, 1972.

"On Death As a Constant Companion," TIME 86:52-53, November 12, 1965.

"On Not Getting Better: Death's Unique Mystery and Its Irreversible Destiny," by Z. M. Cotter HOSP PROG 53: 60-63, March, 1972.

"On the Ambivalence of Death: The Case of the Missing Harlequin," by D. Papageorgis PSYCHOL REP 19:325-326, August, 1966.

"The Only Sure Thing," by E. M. Baxter NURS TIMES 64:
1136, August 23, 1968.

"Other Dimensions of Death," by M. J. Krant PRISM 1:
54-58, July, 1973.

"Pervasive Death: An Avoided Concept," by J. H. Krahn
ED LEAD 31:18-20, October, 1973.

"Predilection to Death," by A. D. Weisman, et al. PSY-
CHOSOM MED 23, 3: 232-256, 1961.

"Problem of the Dying Patient," N Y J MED 5:2356-2366,
September 15, 1965.

"Problems Concerning Death," by J. Brehant NOUV PRESSE
MED 3:609-611, March 9, 1974.

"Problems in the Meaning of Death; AAAS Symposium," by
L. R. Kass SCIENCE 170:1235-1236, December 11, 1970.

"Reactions to Approaching Death," by A. M. Meisel, et
al. DIS NERV SYST 26,1:15-24, January, 1965.

"The Scheme of Life, Yesterday and Tomorrow," BULL IN-
FIRM CATH CAN 46:197-202, September-October, 1969.

"The Sense of Immortality: On Death and the Continuity
of Life," by R. J. Lufton AM J PSYCHOANAL 33:3-15,
1973.

"Separating Ourselves From Death: Excerpt from Art of
Dying," by R. E. Neale NEW CATH WORLD 216:178-182,
July, 1973.

"Soliloquy on Death," by A. Feigenbaum HOSP MGMT 97:10,
June, 1964.

"Soliloquy on Death," by T. Hale HOSP MGMT 97:11, April,
1964.

"Soliloquy on Death," by C. U. Letourneau HOSP MGMT 96:
58+, November, 1963.

"Some Part of Me Will Cheat the Goddess of Death," by
G. G. Murphy NURS TIMES 61:720, May 21, 1965.

"Sounding Board. A 'Will' to Live," by W. Modell NEW
ENG J MED 290:907-908, April 18, 1974.

"The Styx," by B. N. Brooke LANCET 2:96-97, July 13,
1974.

"This He Said, Signifying What Death He Should Die,"
NURS OUTLOOK 16:19, October, 1968.

"This Issue of Dying," by M. J. Howe ANA REG CLIN CONF
6:24-32, 1965.

"Thoughts Regarding the Meaning of Death," by S. A.
Plummer J PASTORAL CARE 21:24-34, March, 1967.

"A Time to Die: Further Reflections," MED J AUST 1:127-
128, January 18, 1969.

"A Time to Die: Further Reflections," by J. Woolnough
MED J AUST 1:427, February 22, 1969.

"To Beat or Not to Beat: That Is the Question," by W.
B. Frommeyer, Jr. ALA J MED SCI 10:318-320, July, 1973.

"To Everything There Is a Season and a Time to Every
Purpose," by F. S. Wald NEW PHYS 18:278-285, April,
1969.

"Toward a Better Death: Views of A. Weisman," TIME 99:
60-61, June 5, 1972.

"Undiscovered Country," by H. C. Meserve SAT R 44:43-44,
March 4, 1961.

"A Voce Velata Discourse -- Life and Death; or, Whither
Do We Wander?" by D. Cri TUBERCULOLOGY 22:10-12, September, 1964.

"What Does It Mean to Die? A Conversation in Sicily," by
D. Dolci HUDSON R 17:167-186, Summer, 1964.

DEATH: MEANING OF

"What Man Shall Live and Not See Death?" NO 12:23, January, 1964.

"When Death Is Inexorable," by R. A. Andree, et al. SCIENCE 169:717, August 21, 1970.

"Work for the Night Is Coming," by L. P. Hudson REPORTER 28:48-49, January 17, 1963.

DEATH: STYLES OF DYING
"One Hundred Deaths in Practice," J. R. Caldwell J R COLL GEN PRACT 21:460-468, August, 1971.

"Styles of Dying: Taxonomy and Correlates," by M. M. Castles MO NURSE 40:10, December, 1971.

"Three Processes of Dying and Their Behavioral Effects," by K. A. Chandler J CONSULT PSYCH 29:296-301, 1965.

"Way of Dying," ATLAN 199:53-535, January, 1957.Discussion 199:30+, March, 1957.

"Way of Dying," READ DIG 70:137-139, March, 1957, Discussion 70:250-252, June, 1957.

DEATH: TIME
"As the Clock Runs Out," by R. Kastenbaum MENT HYG 50: 332-336, July, 1966.

"Effect of Stressful Physical Illness on Future Time Perspective," by A. L. Porter, et al. J CLIN PSYCHOL 27:447-448, October, 1971.

"Extension of Personal Time, Affective States, and Expectation of Personal Death," by P. Wohlford J PERSON SOC PSYCH 3:559-566, May, 1966.

"Heaven . . . It So Quickly Comes," by J. Decker PN 15:28+, December, 1965.

"In the Hour of Their Going Forth," by H. MacLaurin SOC CASEW 40:136-141, March, 1959. Reply. 40:395, July, 1959.

DEATH: TIME

"The Last Hour Before Death," by M. Walker AM J NURS
73:1592-1593, September, 1973.

"Thursday Afternoon at Lunch," by F. V. Sibbers AM J
NURS 74:1308-1309, July, 1974.

"Time, Death and Eternal Life," C. Hartshorne J RELIG
32:97-107, April, 1952.

"The Time of Death," by R. J. Jolling AZ MED 30:159-
163, March, 1973.

"A Time to Die," by E. Gillette POINT VIEW 10:17-18,
#1, 1973.

"A Time to Die," by Lewis NURS FORUM 4:7+, #1, 1965.

"A Time to Live and a Time to Die," by C. Henry NURS
TIMES 67:1016-1018, August 19, 1971.

DEATH: TRANSPLANTS
"Life, Death, and Heart Transplantations," by D. Peters
AORN J 9:38-41, April, 1969.

DEATH AND DYING: EXPERIENCE OF
"Death in the First Person," AM J NURS 70:336, February,
1970.

"The Experience of Dying," by R. Noyes, Jr. PSYCHIAT 35:
174-184, May, 1972.

"The Experience of Dying," by E. M. Pattison AM J PSYCH-
OTHERAP 21:32-43, January, 1967.

"Great Adventure," by J. Boley LADIES HOME J 76:45+,
January, 1959.

"How It Feels to Die," by D. Snell LIFE May 26, 1967.

"On the Experience of Nearly Dying," by R. C. Hunter AM
J PSYCHIAT 124:84-88, July, 1967.

"One Wants to Know How It Really Is to Die," by A. Anders-
sson TIDSKR SVER SJUKSKOT 41:48-49, May 3, 1974.

"Pleasures of Dying: Experience of Almost Dying," TIME 100:62+, December 4, 1972.

"Portion of Thyself," by A. Silberman READ DIG 90:157-160, March, 1967.

"The Ultimate Adventure," by J. P. Warbasse GERIAT 11: 468-469, 1956.

"What Is Dying Like?" by M. A. Simpson NURS TIMES 69: 405-406, March, 1973.

"What Is It Like to Be Dying?" by E. K. Ross AM J NURS 71:54-61, January, 1971.

"What Is It Like to Be Dying?" by E. K. Ross JAP J NURS ART 18:134-145, May, 1972.

"What Is It Like to Be Dying?" E. K. Ross KANGO 23:50-58, April, 1971.

"Where Is Thy Sting?" by J. Lydgate SPEC 206:308, March 3, 1961.

"Who Is to Say?" by P. Breen AM J NURS 67:1689-1690, August, 1967.

"Wonderful Experience," TIME 68:59, August 27, 1956.

"Word," by V. P. McCorry AMERICA 94:722, March 31, 1956.

"Word," by V. P. McCorry AMERICA 97:658; September 21, 1957.

"Word," by V. P. McCorry AMERICA 98:254, November 23, 1957.

DEATH WISH
"Age, Personality, and Health Correlates of Death Concerns in Normal Aged Individuals," by P. J. Rhudick, et al. J GERONT 16:44-49, January, 1961.

"Black Leaders and the Wish to Die," by J. Meredith EBONY 28:154-159, May, 1973.

"A Clinical Study of the Role of Hostility and Death
Wishes by the Family and Society in Suicidal Attempts,"
by J. Richman, et al. ISR ANN PSYCHIAT 8:213-231,
December, 1970.

"Death by Chance, Death by Choice," by D. C. Maguire
ATLAN 233:56-65, January, 1974.

"Death by Chance, Death by Choice," by D. C. Maguire
NURS DIG 2:36-42, October, 1974.

"Death by Suggestion: A Critical Note," by T. X. Barber
PSYCHOSOM MED 23:153-155, 1961.

"Death Drive, Ambivalence, and Narcissism," by K. R.
Eissler PSYCHOANAL STUD CHILD 26:25-78, 1971.

"The Death Drive. Aporia of a Monestic Anthropology,
Expression for the Failure of Human Self-Realization,"
by N. Schneemann Z PSYCHOTHER MED PSYCHOL 23:224-233,
November, 1973.

"Death Instinct and Western Man," by F. C. Palmer HIBBERT
J 51:329-337, July, 1953.

"The Death Instinct of Heinrich von Kleist," by G. Schmidt
MUNCH MED WOCHENSCHR 112:758-763, April 17, 1970.

"Death Suggestion," by T. X. Barber PSYCHOSOM MED 23, 2:
153-155, 1961.

"In Spells, Sorcery and the Will to Die," by R.J. Burrell
MED WORLD NEWS II:(25),33-34, 1961.

"Man's Determination of His Time of Illness or Death.
Anniversary Reactions and Emotional dedline," by H.
K. Fischer, et al. GERIAT 26:89-94, July, 1971.

"On Love and the Death-Drive," by F. X. Schupper AM IMAGO
21:3-10, Fall, 1964.

"On Social Regression (Existence of a Death Instinct),"
by P. E. Slater AM SOC REV 28:339-364, June, 1963.

"On the Death Instinct," by S. Viderman REV FRANC PSYCH-ANAL 25:89-129, January-February, 1961.

"Predilection to Death," by A. D. Weisman, et al. PSYCHOSOM MED 23:232-255, 1961.

"A Psychologi-al Setting of Somatic Disease: The Giving-Up -- Given-Up Complex," by G. L. Engel PROC ROY SOC MED 60:553-555, 1967.

"Reality and Clinical Significance of Death Drives," by S. Biran PSYCHOTHER PSYCHOSOM 19:129-159, 1971.

"Self-Willed Death," by N. B. Levy LANCET 2:496, September 1, 1973.

"Self-Willed Death or the Bone Pointing Syndrome," by G. W. Milton LANCET 1:1435-1436, June 23, 1973.

"So-Called 'Death Instinct'," by I. A. Caruso SCHWEIZ ARCH NEUROL   PSYCHIAT 70:245-258, 1952.

"Submissive Death: Giving Up on Life," by M. E. P. Seligman PSYCHOL TODAY 7:80-85, May, 1974.

"Suicide and Natural Death in a State Hospital Population: A Comparison of Admission Complaints, MMPI Profiles, and Social Competence Factors," by M. R. Ravensborg, et al. J CONSULT CLIN PSYCHOL 33:466-471, August, 1969.

"Terminal Death-Wish," by M. Bernier CATH HOSP #4, March 8, 1970.

"Thoughts About Death and Death Instinct. Apropos of Some More or Less Recent Books," by M. Eck PRESSE MED 77:1829-1832, November 22, 1969.

"Within the Realm of the Death Drive," by A. Garma PSYCHE 25:433-451, June-July, 1971.

"Within the Realm of the Death Instinct," by A. Garma INT J PSYCHOANAL 52:145-154, 1971.

DENTISTS

"Community Dentistry's Contributions to Oral Care of the Aged and Patients in Terminal Illness," by C. O. Dummett J AM COLL DENT 38:152-160, July, 1971.

"Prosthetic Management of Terminal Canver Patients,' by R. Cantor, et al.   PROSTH DENT 20:361-366, October, 1968.

DOCTORS: ATTITUDES OF
"The Act of Death, the Art of Treatment," by R. Noyes MED INSIGHT 3:22-23+, March, 1971.

"The Anesthesiologist in Patient Care," by K. M. Janis JAMA 212:629, April 27, 1970.

"Attitude of Medical Residents Toward the Dying Patient in a General Hospital," by T. Rich, et al. POSTGRAD MED 40, 4:a127-130, October, 1966.

"Attitude of the Physician in the Presence of Cardio-respiratory Failure," by P. H. Benavides GAC MED MEX 106:101-103, August, 1973.

"Attitude of the Physician Towards the Patient in the Terminal Phase. Concept of Life," by H. Jinich GAC MED MEX 106:96-100, August, 1973.

"The Attitudes of Physicians Toward Prolonging Life," by T. A. Travis, et al. PSYCHIAT   MED 5:17-26, Winter, 1974.

"Attitude Survey of Iowa Physicians," by Noyes, et al. ARCH INTERN MED 132:607-611, October, 1973.

"Coping with a Job You Dread," by E. Kubler-Ross HOSP PHYS 9:30+, April, 1973.

"Dealing with Death: Thanatology Looks at the Doctor and the Dying Patient," by M. Weber MED WORLD NEWS 12: 30-36, May 21, 1971.

"Death and Doctors," by K. S. Jones MED J AUST 49(2): 329-334, September 1, 1962.

"Death and Dying: Attitudes of Patient and Doctor. 3
Attitudes of Patients with Advanced Malignancy," by
S. L. Feder GROUP ADVANCE PSYCHIAT (Sympos) 5:614-
622, October, 1965.

"Death and the Doctor," by B. L. MacKinnon J MAINE MED
ASS 63:169-171, August, 1972.

"Death and the Physician," by A. Bourguignon SEM HOP
INFORM 22:2-3, May 14, 1963.

"Death and Nursing. 7. Clinical Course of Death. (2).
Personal Involvement of the Physician Beyond the Pro-
fessional Level Causing Friction with the Family," by
H. Kono JAP J NURS 37:904-910, July, 1973.

"Death, Life and the Medical Profession," by J. Voight
T SYGEPL 67:13-15, January, 1967.

"Do We Need Restraint in Medicine?" by W. D. Poe
CHR CENT 90:914-918, September 19, 1973.

"Doctor and the Dying Patient," by L. Lasagna J CHRON
DIS 22:65-68, July, 1969.

"Doctor Looks at Death," by M. Goldberg MED WORLD NEWS
15:52, September 6, 1974.

"Doctor Looks at Death," by F. Marti-Ibanez READ DIG
84:145-146+, March, 1964.

"The Doctor, the Dying Patient, and the Bereaved," by
J. R. Marshall, et al. ANN INTERN MED 70:615-620,
March, 1969.

"Doctors and Dying," by R. J. Bulger ARCH INTERN MED
112:327-332, September, 1963.

"Doctors and the Dying Patient," EMERG MED 5:204-205,
January, 1973.

"Doctors, Death, and the Truth," DEL MED J 41:167, May,
1969.

"The Dying Patient and His Doctor," by R. Bulger HARV-
ARD MED ALUM BULL 34:23-25, 53-57, 1960.

"The Dying Patient, His Physician and the Psychiatric
Consultant," by W. Hicks, et al. PSYCHOSOM 9:47-52,
June-February, 1968.

"Family Doctor at the Death-Bed," by T. N. Rudd MED
WORLD 85:50-52, July, 1956.

"The General Practitioner and the Care of the Dying
Patient," by P. J. Turner S AFR MED J 48:708-710,
April 6, 1974.

"Help for the Young Physician with Death and Grieving,"
by M. D. Kerstein SURG GYNECOL OBSTET 137:479-480,
September, 1973.

"How Can a Physician Prepare His Patient for Death?" by
W. C. Goff JAMA 201:280, July 21, 1967.

"Initial Responses to Grief: The Physician's Problems
and Opportunities," by R. E. Buxbaum TEX MED 70:94-98,
February, 1974.

"Is Death's Sting Sharper for the Doctor?" MED WORLD
NEWS 8:77, October 6, 1967.

"Life and Death and the Physician," by J. R. Elkinton
ANN INTERN MED 67:669, September, 1967.

"Life, Death, and the Family\Physician," by H. S. Abram
VA MED MON 97:222-225, April, 1970.

"On the Physician's Professional Discretion After the
Death of the Patient," by E. Trube-Becker DEUTSCH
Z GES GERICHTL MED 57:36-45, 1966.

"On the Physician-Patient Relation," by G. DeAraujo H
TOP PROBL PSYCHOTHER 4:250-258, 1963.

"The Patient-Physician Relationship," by W. S. Middle-
ton WIS MED J 54:288-292, June, 1955.

"Physician and Cancer Patient," by H. E. Bock   DEUTSCH
MED WSCHR 98:1625-1630, August, 1973.

"The Physician and Death," by F. Dreyfuss HAREFUAH 84: 307-308, March 15, 1973.

"The Physician and Death," by I. Magyar. ORV HETIL 111: 3011-3014, December 20, 1970.

"The Physician and Death in the Arts," by H. Nathan, et al. PROC RUDOLPH VIRCHOW MED SOC CITY NY 27:143-169, 1968-1969.

"The Physician and the Minister Caring for the Terminal Patient," by L. C. Ratliff J MISS STATE MED ASS 13:202-207, May, 1972.

"The Physician and the Cancer Patient," by S. G. Taylor, et al. JAMA 150:1012-1015, 1952.

"Physician and the Dying Patient," by G. Tourney NW MED 68:1133-1138, December, 1969.

"The Physician and the Terminal Patient," by A. B. Scoville, Jr. J TENN MED ASS 58:208-209, June, 1965.

"The Physician and the End of Life," by E. Ansohn WIEN MED WSCHR 118:1025-1029, November 30, 1968.

"The Physician As Witness the Problem of Dying Declarations," W. Charyk MED ANN DC 41:641-642, October, 1972.

"Physician at Bedside of Incurable Patient," by H. R. Bax NED TIDJDSCHR GENEESKD 100:2601-2610, September 8, 1956.

"The Physician Facing the Frontier of Death," by F. Lamas REV ESP ANESTESIOL REANIM 21:112-126, March, 1974.

"A Physician Looks at Death," by F. W. Sunderman ASS CLIN LAB SCI 3:393-398, September-October, 1973.

"Physician Management of Dying Patients: An Exploration," by H. J. Friedman PSYCHIAT MED 1:295-305, October, 1970.

"The Physician, the Child and Death. I, The Pediatrician's Point of View," by J. Weill REV MED PSYCHOSOM
10:407-417, October-December, 1968.

"Physician, the Nurse, and the Dying Patient," by F. P.
Kosbab NEW PHYS 17:50-52, February, 1968.

"The Physician, the Patient and Suffering," by L.
Goulet LAVAL MED 40:655-658, September, 1969.

"The Physician's Management of the Dying Patient," by
C. W. Wahl CURR PSYCHIAT THERAP 2:127-136, 1962.

"Physician's Role Examined," by Krant PRISM 1:55-58,
July, 1973.

"The Physician's Responsibility to the Dying Patient,"
by R. C. Lippincott MED CLIN N AM 56:677-680, May,
1972.

"The Physician's Role in Terminal Illness and Death,"
by L. Christenson MINNMED 46:881-883, September, 1963.

"The Physican's Treatment of the Dying Patient," by C.
W. Wahl ANN NY ACAD SCI 164:759-775, December 19,
1969.

"Physicians and Death," by L. Feigenberg LAKARTIDNINGEN
68:6103-6112, December 22, 1971.

"Physicians and the Bereaved," by B. B. Schoenberg, et
al. GP 40:105-108, October, 1969.

"Physicians Fear Death," SCI N L 80:166, September 9,
1961.

"Physicians Help to Advance Hypocrisy About Death," by
L. S. Kolmos NORD MED 89:169, June, 1974.

"The Practicing Physician and Death Research," by R. A.
Kalish MED TIMES 97:211-220, January, 1969.

"Premonition of Death: A Safeguard From Malpractice,"
by A. P. Seltzer J LEG MED 1:28-29, September-October,
1973.

"Preventive Medicine and 'Natural Death'," by G. Bidrek
ACTA MED SCAND 195:441-442, June, 1974.

"Psychologic Considerations in the Management of Deaths
on Pediatric Hospital Services. 1. The Doctor and
the Child's Family," PEDIAT 24:106-112, 1959.

"Relationship of the Physician in Practice to a Children's Cancer Clinic," PEDIAT 40,3(II):537-539, September, 1967.

"The Role of the Surgeon in the Prospect of Death from
Cancer," by D. S. Martin ANN NY ACAD SCI 164:739-748,
December 19, 1969.

"The Role of the Surgeon in the Prospect of Death from
Cancer," by D. S. Martin CA 18:264-267, September-
October, 1968.

"The Self-Image of the Physician and the Care of Dying
Patients," by L. P. White ANN NY ACAD SCI 164:822-
837, December 19, 1969.

"Should We See Our Patients After Death? An Analysis
of 100 Deaths in a Country Practice," by S. M. Evans,
et al. PRACTITIONER 192:805-806, June, 1964.

"Sociocultural Stresses and the Physician-Patient Relationship," JAMA 170,14:1648-1651, August, 1959.

"Southern California University Researchers Hold Fear
of Death Is Why Some Become Doctors," THE NEW YORK
TIMES 19:4, September 4, 1967.

"Survey of Iowa Physicians," by Noyes, et al. J IOWA
MED SOC 63:527-530, November, 1973.

"Treating the Dying Patient," by Henderson CHRIST MED
SOC J 1+, September-October, 1967.

"Treatment of a Dying Patient," by J. Norton PSYCHOANAL
STUD CHILD 18:541-560, 1963.

"What a Dying Man Taught Doctors About Caring," by C.
Driver MED ECON 50:81-86, January 22, 1973.

DOCTORS: DEATH OF

"Dying Doctor Filmed for Medical Students," MED WORLD NEWS 14:54, July 6, 1973.

"Is Death's Sting Sharper for the Doctor?" MED WORLD NEWS 8:77, October 6, 1967.

"The Physician Facing the Frontier of Death," by F. Lamas REV ESP ANESTESIOL REANIM 21:112-126, March, 1974.

"Physicians Fear Death," SCI N L 80:166, September 9, 1961.

"Southern California University Researchers Hold Fear of Death Why Some Choose Medical Careers," THE NEW YORK TIMES 19:4, September 4, 1967.

"When the Doctor Dies," J LOUIS MED SOC 119:324-327, August, 1967.

DRUGS

"Attitudes Toward Death and Dying on a Drug Addiction Unit," by R. Gertler, et al. INT J ADDICT 8:265-272, 1973.

"The Psychadelic 'Hip Scene': Return of the Death Instinct," by H. R. Brickman AM J PSYCHIAT 125:766-772, December, 1968.

DRUGS TO EASE DYING

"Beyond Dying: Use of LSD to Ease the Transition from Life," by J. Avorn HARPER 246:56-60+, March, 1973. Reply with Rejoinder. N. E. Zinberg. 246:113-114, May, 1973.

"Bliss Before Dying?" NEWSWEEK 83:63-64, May 6, 1974.

"Dr. S. Cohen's Experiment to See if LSD Can Lessen Pain of Death," THE NEW YORK TIMES 83:7, October 26, 1967.

"Dr. Kast Reports LSD Eases Fears of Dying Patients," THE NEW YORK TIMES 44:1, June 14, 1966.

"Doctors Attending International Symposium on Drug Care of Dying at Columbia University Conclude That Role Exists for Use . . . (of Drugs)," THE NEW YORK TIMES 1:1, November 13, 1971.

"Drug Treatment of Cancer," by L. A. Price NURS TIMES 68:1412-1413, November 9, 1972.

"Heroin in the Treatment of Incurably Ill Patients," by R. Tybusz, et al. POL TYG LEK 29:1129-1130, July 1, 1974.

"Letter: Euphoriant Elixirs," by R. G. Twycross, et al. BRIT MED J 4:552, December 1, 1973.

"LSD-Assisted Psychotherapy with Terminal Cancer Patients," by W. N. Pahnke, et al. CURR PSYCHIAT THERAP 9:144-152, 1969.

"LSD and the Dying Patient," by E. Kast CHICAGO MED SCH Q 26:80-7, Summer, 1966.

"LSD vs. Death," SCI DIG 75:25, February, 1974.

"Man in Search of Meaning. II. Hallucinogenic Agents," by E. Marcovitz DEL MED J 44:72-74, March, 1972.

"Trip Before Dying," NEWSWEEK 78:67, November 27, 1971.

EDUCATION
SEE ALSO: THANATOLOGY

EDUCATION: ATTITUDES
"Accepting Death As a Fact of Life. In-Service Training," EDUC 2:6, May, 1973.

"Catholic Students Look at Death," by J. J. McMahon COMMONWEAL 87:491-494, January 26, 1968. Reply. F. V. Manning. 88:59+, April 5, 1968.

"Changes in Nursing Student's Attitudes Toward Death and Dying. A Measurement of Curriculum Integration Effectiveness," by M. Snyder, et al. INT J SOC PSYCHIAT 19:294-298, Autumn, 1973.

EDUCATION: CHILDREN

"Catholic Students Look at Death," by J. J. McMahon
COMMONWEAL 87:491-494, January 26, 1968. Reply.
F. V. Manning. 88:59+, April 5, 1968.

"Children Ask About Death," by M. E. Lichtenwalner INT
J RELIG ED 14-16, June, 1965.

"Death Studies Should Begin with Very Young," by J.
McCurdy TIMES ED SUPP 3074:12, April 26, 1974.

"Helping Children to Understand Death: An Experience
with Death in a Nursery School," by M. McDonald J
NURS ED 19: 19-25, November, 1963.

"Miniguide: A Mini-Course on Death," by G. Stanford
SCHOL TEACH JR/SR HIGH 40-44, September, 1973.

"A Program on What Death Means to Children for Your Discussion Group," by M. Smart PARENTS MAG & BETTER HOME-
MAKER 15-16, March, 1965.

"School Workshop on Death," THE NEW YORK TIMES 17:1,
June 25, 1974.

"A Study of Some Psychological Reactions During Prepubescence to the Idea of Death," by F. S. Caprio
PSYCHIAT Q 24, 3: 495-505, 1950.

"What Shall We Teach About Death in Science Classes?"
by J. M. Hair EL SCHL J 65:414-418, May, 1965.

EDUCATION: GENERAL
"ANF Supports Study of Dying Patients," NURS RES REP 5:
2, June, 1970.

"Accepting Death As a Fact of Life,. In-Service Training,"
EDUC 2:6, May, 1973.

"Catholic Students Look at Death," by J. J. McMahon
COMMONWEAL 87:491-494, January 26, 1968. Reply.
F. V. Manning. 88:59+, April 5, 1968.

"Changes in Nursing Student's Attitudes Toward Death
and Dying. A Measurement of Curriculum Integration
Effectiveness," by M. Snyder, et al. INT J SOC PSYCH-
IAT 19:294-298, Autumn, 1973.

"Children Ask About Death," by M. E. Lichtenwalner INT
J RELIG ED 14-16, June, 1965.

"Continuing Education in Death and Dying," by J. A. Thor-
son ADULT LEAD 23:141-144, November, 1974.

"A Course on Death Education and Suicide Prevention:
Implications for Health Education," by D. Leviton J
AM COLL HEALTH ASS 19:217-220, April, 1971.

"Dealing with the Last Chapter of Life," by L. H. Nahum
CONN MED 30:170-174, March, 1966.

"Death: A Concept in Transition," by F. L. Delmonico,
et al. PEDIAT 51:234-239, February, 1973.

"Death and Dying: A Course for Medical Students," by
D. Barton, et al. J MED ED 47:945-951, December, 1972.

"Death and Dying -- It's the Coming Thing," by R. I.
Anders J CONTIN ED NURS 5:45-48, September-October,
1974.

"Death and Dying -- Oncology Discussion Group," by M. P.
Corder, et al. J PSYCHIAT NURS 12:10-14, July-August,
1974.

"Death and the Curriculum," by Drummon, et al. J NURS
ED 1:21-28, May-June, 1962.

"Death and the Student Nurse," by K. Lyons TOM NURS 4:
21-22, October-November, 1963.

"Death Education," by J. W. McLure PHI DELTA KAPPAN 55:
483-485, March, 1974.

"Death Education: An Independent Study Unit," by J. D.
McMahon J SCH HEALTH 43:526-527, October, 1973.

"Death Education As Part of Family Life Education: Us-
ing Imaginative Literature for Insights Into Family
Crises," by R. M. Somerville FAM COORD 20:223-224,
July, 1971.

EDUCATION: GENERAL

"Death -- Everybody's Concern," by U. Jansson TIDSKR
SVER SJUKSKOT 41:3, May 3, 1974.

"Death: No More Taboos," by C. A. Forbes CHR TODAY 16:
41-42, May 26, 1972.

"Death Studies Should Begin with Very Young," by J.
McCurdy TIMES ED SUPP 3074:12, April 26, 1974.

"Death: the Subject We Avoid," by W. T. Eggers PROF
NURS HOME 10:12-13, April, 1968.

"Death's Pedagogy," by P. Ramsey COMMONWEAL 100:497-502,
September 20, 1974.

"Discussions Meet Needs of Dying Patients," by D. A.
Heymann HOSP 48:57-62, July 16, 1974.

"Dr. Gary Leinbach, Dying of Cancer at 39 Videotaped
Messages About Care of the Dying," THE NEW YORK TIMES
1:2, July 22, 1974.

"Does the Dying Patient Have Something to Teach Physi
cians and Nurses?" JAMA 208:951-952, May 12, 1969.

"Dying Is Worked to Death," by S. Vaisrub JAMA 229:1909-
1910, September 30, 1974.

"Dying Patients Teach at Chicago University," AM J NURS
69:922, May, 1969.

"Education for Death: Health Education at the University of Maryland," by D. Leviton JOHPER 40:46-47+,
September, 1969.

"Education of Death and Dying: A Survey of American Medical Schools," by E. H, Liston J MED ED 48:577-578,
June, 1973.

"The Effect of Medical Education on Attitudes: A Follow-
Up Study," by L. Eron J MED ED 33, II:25-33, 1958.

"Explorations in Death Education," by R. E. Neale PAST
PSYCH 22:33-74, November, 1971.

"Great Unmentionable," by C. Driver ATLAS 10:113-114, August, 1965.

"Helping Children to Understand Death: An Experience with Death in a Nursery School," by M. McDonald J NURS ED 19:19-25, November, 1963.

"How to Die," MED J AUST 2:734-735, September 23, 1972.

"How to Live with the Thought of Dying," by C. Saunders SAIRAANHOITAJA 48:719-721, September 25, 1972.

"How We Discuss DEATH in the Adult Health Course for Registered Nurse Students," by E. E. Drummond, et al. J NURS ED 1:21-28, May-June, 1962.

"The Importance of Death Education in Family Life," by D. H. Peniston FAM LIFE COORD 11:15-18, January, 1962.

"Interdisciplinary Approach to Death Education," by J. A. Sadwith J SCHL HEALTH 44:455-458, October, 1974.

"Is Death Our Failure?" by R. Berry J PRACT NURS 24:30+, November, 1974.

"Learning About Death," by G. M. Speer J AM VET MED ASS 165:70-73, August 15, 1974.

"Learning About Death," by G. M. Speer PERSPECT PSYCH-IAT CARE 12:70-73, April-June, 1974.

"Learning About Dying," by D. J. Wise NURS OUTLK 22: 42-44, January, 1974.

"Learning From a Dying Patient," by J. Carson A, J NURS 71:333-334, February, 1971.

"Learning How to Die," by D. Dempsey THE NEW YORK TIMES MAG 58+, November 14, 1971, Discussion, 125, December 5, 1971.

"Learning to Die," by E. J. Cassell BULL NY ACAD MED 49: 1110-1118, December, 1973.

"Learning to Die," by T. Powers HARPER 242:72-74+,
June, 1971.

"A Lesson for the Living," Z KRANKENPFL 63:433-434,
December, 1970.

"A Lesson From a Gentleman," by Marino PN 17:26+, August, 1967.

"Lesson in Dying: Television Film Shows Life Coming to
an End," LIFE 65:107-108, December 13, 1968.

"Lessons From a Dying Patient," by D. Sharp AM J NURS
68:1517-1520, July, 1968.

"Lessons of Death," CHR TODAY 18:31, January 18, 1974.

"Lessons of Sorrow," by J. E. Brown BET HOME & GARD 30:
109+, November, 1952.

"Let the Dead Teach the Living," by J. D. Ratcliff READ
DIG 87-90, August, 1961.

"Let Us Talk About Death," by J. Viorst REDBOOK 141:33-
34, June, 1973.

"Let's Talk About Death. To Overcome Inhibiting Emotions," by R. L. Vanden Bergh AM J NURS 66:71-73,
January, 1966.

"Lies Can Save Lives," J MED SOC N J 66:646, December,
1969.

"Lifting the Darkness of Death," by M. B. Johnstone
CORONET 27:52-56, March, 1950.

"Listening to the Dying," NURS TIMES 69:16, January
4, 1973.

"Live Issues Surrounding Death Education," by D. R.
Crase, et al. J SCH HEALTH 44:70-73, February, 1974.

"Living with the Dying," NEWSWEEK 84:89, December 2, 1974.

"Living with the Dying," by J. Brimigion NURS'72
2:23-27, June, 1972.

"Making of a Successful Seminar on Death and Dying," by
F. W. Carris VOL LEAD 15:9-11, November, 1974.

"A Mental Health Seminar on Facing Death," by M.
Katajamakl SAIRAANHOITAJA 50:9-11, July 9, 1974.

"Miniguide: A Mini-Course on Death," by G. Stanford
SCHOL TEACH JR/SR HIGH 40-44, September, 1973.

"NYU Offers Course, The Meaning of Death," THE NEW YORK
TIMES 70:1, February 14, 1971.

"The Need for Education on Death and Suicide," by D.
Leviton J SCH HEALTH 39:270-274, April, 1969.

"Need for Including Instruction on Death and Dying in
the Medical Curriculum," by D. Barton J MED ED 47:169-
175, March, 1972.

"Nobody Had Really Talked About Dying," by D. E. Welk
RN 36:ICU/CCU 1+, November, 1973.

"Notes of a Dying Professor," NURS OUTLK 20:502-506,
August, 1972.

"Notes of a Dying Professor," by A. J. Hanlan NURS DIG
2:36-42, May, 1974.

"Nurse Training," by J. McTrusty BRIT MED J 1:38, January, 1973.

"Nurses Need Training in Terminal Care," by F. L. Mc-
Quillan MOD NURS HOME 22:83+, May-June, 1968.

"On the Outside -- Looking In," by M. B. King NURS TIMES
66:542-543, April 23, 1970.

"Physical Education and Death," by W. E. Warren PHYS ED
28:127-128, October, 1971.

"Playing Ostrich," by T. J. Lincoln JAMA 219:1764-1765,
March 27, 1972.

"Preparing Nurses to Care for the Fatally Ill," by J.
C. Quint INT J NURS STUD 5:53-59, March, 1968.

"Profound Lessons for the Living," by L. Wainwright LIFE
67:35-43, November 21, 1969.

"A Program on What Death Means to Children for Your Discussion Group," by M. Smart PARENTS MAG & BETTER HOME-
MAKER 15-16, March, 1965.

"Proposed Model to Teach Medical Students the Care of
the Dying Patient," by H. S. Olin J MED ED 47:564-
567, July, 1972.

"Psychiatric Aspects of Life-Threatening Illness: A
Course for Medical Students, " by E. H. Liston PSY-
CHIAT MED 5:51-56, Winter, 1974.

"Questions of Life and Death," by N. Hershey AM J NURS
68:1910-1912, September, 1968.

"Randy -- the Silent Teacher,' by S. Nau, et al. CAN
NURS 61:903-906, November, 1965.

"Report on Seminar on the Care of the Dying," by Eucharia
IRISH NURS NEWS 2-5, January-February, 1966.

"Remarkable Television Film: Lesson in Dying," LIFE 65:
107-108, December 13, 1968.

"Research on Understanding Death at Billings Memorial
Hospital," THE NEW YORK TIMES 6:58, November 14, 1971.

"School Workshop on Death," THE NEW YORK TIMES 17:1,
June 25, 1974.

"The Sense of Being Dead and of Dying: Some Perspectives,"
by I. Fast, et al. J PROJECT TECHN 34:190-193, June,
1970.

"Some Lessons on Dying," by B. Hale CHR CENT 88:1076-
1079, September 15, 1971.

"Subject Nobody Teaches," by C. Fontenot ENG J 63:62-63, February, 1974.

"Survey of Medical School Education on Death and Dying," by Liston J MED ED 48:577-578, June, 1973.

"Stevens Park Osteopathic Hospital Trains Employees on Dealing with Dying Patients," OSTEO HOSP 17:30, October, 1973.

"Study of Dying is Necessary," by W. Schweisheimer KRAN-KENPFLEGE 26:338, August, 1972.

"Summaries of Selected Works on Death and Dying," by C. Gratton HUMANITAS 10:87-103, February, 1974.

"TV Film on Death of Ted Rosenthal," THE NEW YORK TIMES 51:1, July 15, 1974.

"Talking About Death," BRIT MED J 2:131-132, April 20, 1974.

"Teaching About Death," by D. W. Berg , et al. TODAYS ED 62:46-47, March, 1973.

"Teaching About Death and Dying," NURS TIMES 69:442-443, April 5, 1973.

"Teaching Nurses to Care for the Dying Patient," by N. Sanford, et al. J PSYCHIAT NURS 11:24-26, January-February, 1973.

"Teaching Psychiatry in the Context of Dying and Death," by D. Barton AM J PSYCHIAT 130:1290-1291, November, 1973.

"Teaching Students to Work With the Dying," by B. M. Wagner AM J NURS 64:128-131, November, 1964.

"To Be a Strong Hand in the Dark," by P. Goodwin NURS TIMES 62:782, June 10, 1966.

"What Shall We Teach About Death in Science Classes?" by J. M. Hair EL SCHL J 65:414-418, May, 1965.

"Death and Dying: A Course for Medical Students," by D. Barton, et al. J MED ED 47:945-951, December, 1972.

"Education of Death and Dying: A Survey of American Medical Schools," by E. H. Liston J MED ED 48:577-578, June, 1973.

"The Effect of Medical Education on Attitudes: A Follow-Up Study," by L. Eron J MED ED 33,II:25-33, 1958.

"Need for Including Instruction on Death and Dying in the Medical Curriculum," by D. Barton J MED ED 47:169-175, March, 1972.

"Proposed Model to Teach Medical Students the Care of the Dying Patient," by H. S. Olin J MED ED 47:564-567, July, 1972.

"Psychiatric Aspects of Life-Threatening Illness: A Course for Medical Students," by E. H. Liston PSY-CHIAT MED 5:51-56, Winter, 1974.

"Survey of Medical School Education on Death and Dying," by E. H. Liston J MED ED 48:577-578, June, 1973.

EDUCATION: NURSES

"Discussions Meet Needs of Dying Patients," by D. A. Heymann HOSP 48:57-62, July 16, 1974.

"Does the Dying Patient Have Something to Teach Physicians and Nurses?" JAMA 208:951-952, May 12, 1969.

"How We Discuss Death in the Adult Health Course for Registered Nurse Students," by E. E. Drummond, et al. J NURS ED 1:21-28, May-June, 1962.

"Nurse Training," by J. McTrusty BRIT MED J 1:38, January, 1973.

"Nurses Need Training in Terminal Care," by F. L. McQuillan MOD NURS HOME 22:83+, May-June, 1968.

"Preparing Nurses to Care for the Fatally Ill," by J. C. Quint INT J NURS STUD 5:53-59, March, 1968.

EDUCATION: NURSES

"Teaching Nurses to Care for the Dying Patient," by N.
Sanford, et al. J PSYCHIAT NURS 11:24-26, January-
February, 1973.

EDUCATION: NURSING STUDENTS
"Changes in Nursing Student's Attitudes Toward Death
and Dying. A Measurement of Curriculum Integration
Effectiveness," by M. Snyder, et al. INT J SOC PSYCH-
IAT 19:294-298, Autumn, 1973.

"Death and the Student Nurse," by K. Lyons TOM NURS 4:
21-22, October-November, 1963.

"How we discuss Death in the Adult Health Course for
Registered Nurse Students," by E. E. Drummond, et al.
J NURS ED 1:21-28, May-June, 1962.

"Nurse Training," by J. McTrusty BRIT MED J 1:38, January, 1973.

"Nurses Need Training in Terminal Care," by F. L. Mc-
Quillan MOD NURS HOME 22:83+, May-June, 1968.

"Preparing Nurses to Care for the Fatally Ill," by J.
C. Quint INT J NURS STUD 5:53-59, March, 1968.

"Teaching Nurses to Care for the Dying Patient," by N.
Sanford, et al. J PSYCHIAT NURS 11:24-26, January-
February, 1973.

"Teaching Students to Work with the Dying," by B. M.
Wagner AM J NURS 64:128-131, November, 1964.

EDUCATION: STAFF
"Accepting Death As a Fact of Life. In-Service Training,
EDUC 2:6, May, 1973.

"Dr. Gary Leinbach, Dying of Cancer at 39, Videotaped
Messages About Care of the Dying," THE NEW YORK TIMES
1:2, July 22, 1974.

"Stevens Park Osteopathic Hospital Trains Employees on
Dealing with Dying Patients," OSTEO HOSP 17:30, October, 1973.

124

"Advantage of Being Frank," by R. E. Waggener NEB MED
J 57:316-318, August, 1972.

"All Terminally Ill Patients Can't Handle the Bad News,"
JAMA 229:123, July 8, 1974.

"Am I Going to Dies?" by I. Wolff RN 25:91-96, September,
1962.

"Art of Breaking Bad News," by T. P. Hackett MED ECON
44:130+, June 12, 1967.

"Bedside Ethics for the Hopeless Case," by F. J. Ingelfinger NEW ENG J MED 289:914-915, October 25, 1973.

"Breaking the Bad News," PHYS MANAG 9:81s+, June, 1969.

"Breaking the News of Death," by P. L. Levin THE NEW
YORK TIMES MAGAZINE, February 21, 1965.

"Bolstering the Defenses of the Dying Patient," by Wahl
HOSP PHYS 5:160+, March, 1969.

"The Cancer Patient, His Changing Pattern of Communication," by R. D. Abrams NEW ENG J MED 274:397-422, 1966.

"Communication with the Fatally Ill," by A. Verwoerdt
CA 15:105-111, May-June, 1965.

"Communication with the Fatally Ill," by A. Verwoerdt
S MED J 57:787-795, July, 1964.

"Communication with Fatally Ill Patients. Tacit or Explicit?" by A. Verwoerdt, et al. AM J NURS 67:2307-2309,
November, 1967.

"Communication and Comfort for the Dying Patient," by
E. E. Drummond NURS CLIN N AM 5:55-63, March, 1970.

"Comment on Husband's Death from Cancer and Need to
Discuss His Death and Dying," THE NEW YORK TIMES 167:
3, December 8, 1974.

"Conversations with the Dying," by W. Becher, et al.
DTSCH KRANKENPFLEGEZ 25:600-607, November, 1972.

"Cues to Communication with the Terminal Cancer Patient," by K. B. Heusinkveld NURS FORUM 11:105-113, 1972.

"Death and Nursing. 3. Patient's Right to Know the Truth 1," by H. Kono JAP J NURS 37:370-375, March, 1973.

"Death and Nursing. 4. The Patient's Right to Know the Truth. (2)," by H. Kono JAP J NURS 37:504-508, April, 1973.

"Disclosure of Terminal Illness," by B. G. Glaser J HEAL HUM BEHAV 7:83-91, Summer, 1966.

"Doctors Urged to Tell Fatally Ill Patients of Oncoming Death," THE NEW YORK TIMES 1:6, January 9, 1966.

"Doctor-Patient Relation in Severe Illness: A Seminar for Oncology Fellows," by K. L. Artiss, et al. NEW ENG J MED 288:1210-1214, June 7, 1973.

"Doctor's Dilemma -- What Should the Cancer Patient Be Told?" by A. F. Hartman, Jr. NEW PHYS 18:550-551, July, 1969.

ETHICS: TELLING THE PATIENT

"Advantage of Being Frank," by R. E. Waggener NEB MED J 57:316-318, August, 1972.

"Art of Breaking Bad News," by T. P. Hackett MED ECON 44:130+, June 12, 1967.

"Breaking the Bad News," PHYS MANAG 9:81s+, June, 1969.

"Breaking the News of Death," by P. L. Levin THE NEW YORK TIMES MAGAZINE, February 21, 1965.

"Communication with Fatally Ill Patients. Tacit or Explicit?" by A. Verwoerdt, et al. AM J NURS 67:2307-2309, November, 1967.

"Communication and Comfort for the Dying Patient," by E. E. Drummond NURS CLIN N AM 5:55-63, March, 1970.

"The Dying and Ethics," by B. van Schagen TIJDSCHR ZIE-KENVERPL 25:1140, October 31, 1972.

"Dying Patient Often Not Told," GERIAT 25:25+, July, 1970.

"Emotional Care of Cancer Patient. To Tell or Not to Tell," by F. Rosner NY STATE J MED 74:1467-1469, July, 1974.

"Ethical Implications of the Physician in Relation to Patients in the Terminal Phase," by E. Ruiz-Amezcua GAC MED MEX 106:103-110, August, 1973.

"Ethical Questions in the Care of the Dying," by R. Lamerton NURS MIRROR 139:61-63, October 10, 1974.

"Ethics and Death," by D. Mullan IRISH NURS NEWS 10-1, March-April, 1970.

"Explanation to the Patient," by M. Aasterud NURS FORUM 2,4:36-44, 1963.

"Fatal Illness: Should the Patient Be Told?" by N. B. Levy MED INSIGHT 5:20-23, November, 1973.

"Georgetown University Will Establish Institute to Study Ethical Questions in the Care of Dying Patients," WASH POST 1+, October 2, 1971.

"Guardedness or Openness on the Cancer Unit," by D. Pienschke NURS RES 22:484-490, November-December, 1973.

"How Can a Physician Prepare His Patient for Death?" by W. F. Goff JAMA 201:280, July 21, 1967.

"How Do You Talk with a Dying Patient?" by M. Wexler, et al. HOSP PHYS 10:90-95, February, 1974.

"Impending Death: A Conspiracy of Silence?" by M. F. Ondrouch-Luna RES-INTERN CONS 1:16-17, May, 1972.

"Informing the Patient with Fatal Illness," by A. Verwoerdt POSTGRAD MED 40:A95-99, December, 1966.

"The Initial Contact with the Cancer Patient -- Some Psychiatric Considerations," by R. S. Blacher, et al. J MOUNT SINAI HOSP NY 35: 423-428, July-August, 1968.

"Let's Talk About Death -- to Oversome Inhibiting Emotions," by VandenBergh AJN 66:71+, January, 1966.

"Life, Dying, Death: Ethics and Open Decisions," by A. Etzioni SCI N 106:109+, August 17, 1974.

"Must a Doctor Hide His Conscience?" by D. Scarano HOSP PHYS 3:92-93, August, 1967.

"Must We Reveal to the Patient His Approaching Death?" by J. Brehant, et al. PRESSE MED 79:1300-1302, June 5, 1971.

"Must One Reveal to the Patient His Proxwmate Death?" by E. Lesage-Desrousseaux, et al. SEM HOP PARIS 46: 117-124, January 8, 1970.

"Nothing But the Truth? The Doctor's Dilemma," by I. Ross FAM HEALTH 2:34-35, August, 1970.

"Nursing Ethics: The admirable Professional Standards of Nurses: A Survey report," NURS '74 4:56-66, October, 1974.

"Patient with a Fatal Illness -- To Tell or Not to Tell," by A. H. Becker, et al. JAMA 201:646-648, August 21, 1967.

"The Patient's Right to Know the Truth," by A. Miller CAN NURS 58,1:25-29, January, 1962.

"Patients Can Face Hard Truths, MD Finds," MED WORLD NEWS 6,5:64-65, February 12, 1965.

"The Physician's Role in Terminal Illness and Death," by L. Christenson MINN MED J 46:881-883, September, 1963.

"Physicians, Clergymen and the Privileged Communication," by W. J. Fogelman JAMA 200,6:235, May 8, 1967.

"Playing Supergod: How Should We Tell a Patient with a Fatal Disease?" JAMA 218:588, October 25, 1971.

"Quandry: the Truth or Not?" NURS TIMES 70:48, January 10, 1974.

"The Question of Honesty," by W. H. Young PASTORAL CARE 14,2:65-77, Summer, 1960.

"Questions Reason for Telling Truth to Dying Patients," OR REPORTER 9:1, August, 1974.

"Reactions of Cancer Patients on Being Told Their Diagnosis," by J. Aitken-Swan, et al. BRIT MED J 1:779-783, 1959.

"Diagnosis: CA ... Should We Tell the Truth?" by L. B. Pemberton BULL AM COLL SURG 56:7-13, March, 1971.

"Should a Mentally Alert Old Person Who Is Fatally Ill Be Told He's Going to Die?" GERIAT 25:54+, January, 1970.

"Should a Physician Advise the Patient of an Incurable and Mortal Malignancy?" by J. S. Montedonico MEMPH MED J 32:403-405, December, 1957.

"Should a Physician Tell a Fatally Ill Patient the Truth About His Condition or Should He Keep It Quiet?" by A. Grosswiele DTSCH KRANKENPFLEGEZ 24:561, November, 1971.

"Should Patients Be Tols They Have Cancer," by O. H. Wangensteen SURGERY 27:944-947, 1950.

"Should Patients Be Told When the Diagnosis Is Cancer?" by O. R. Bowen IND ST MED ASS 46,4:303-309, April, 1953.

"Should the Cancer Patient Be Told?" by E. Litin POST-GRAD MED 28:470-475, November, 1960.

"Should the Cancer Patient Be Told?" by J. G. Wilders JAMA 200:733, May 22, 1967.

"Should the Doctor Tell the Patient the Truth? by K. H. Stauder, et al. MED KLIN 48:403-405, 1953.

"Should the Patient Be Told the Truth?" by P. Brauer NURS OUTLK 8, 12:672-676, December, 1960.

"Should the Truth Be Told?" by M. E. Alberts J IOWA MED SOC 63:486, October, 1973.

"Should We Tell the Truth?" by L. B. Pemberton RES STAFF PHYS 18:17s+, May, 1972.

"Silent Conspiration Feels Bitter for the Patient Who Lies Dying," LAKARTIDNINGEN 66:3243, August 13, 1969.

"Talking to Patients About Death," by J. Q. Benoliel NURS FORUM 9:254-268, 1970.

"Talking with People About to Die," by J. Hinton BRIT MED J 3:25-27, July 6, 1974.

"Talking with Persons Who Have Cancer," by J. K. Craytor AM J NURS 69:744-748, April, 1969.

"Talks with Dying Patients," by R. Lindner MED KLIN 68: 975-978, July 20, 1973.

"Tell the Truth to the Patient?" by A. Selvini MINERVA MED 62:1985-1990, May 16, 1971.

"Telling Patients," by Saunders DIST NURS 8:149+, September, 1965.

"Telling Your Child About Death,: by B. Spock LADIES H J 77:14, 1960.

"Temper Forthrightness to the Cancer Patient with Compassion," by M. L. Canick SURG GYN OBSTET 130:886-887, May 7, 1970.

"They Will Talk Again," by W. Gardner NURS OUTLK 2,6: 314-315, June, 1954.

"Thoughts on What to tell a Patient with Cancer," by S. O. Hoerr CLEVE CLIN Q 30:11, 1963.

"Truth and the Dying," by J. M. Cameron SPEC 193:81,
July 16, 1954; Discussion. 193:112, 142, 168, 195,
224, 253, July 23-August 27, 1954.

"Truth versus Illusion in Relation to Death," by R.
Levin PSYCHOANAL REV 51:190-200, Summer, 1964.

"To Tell or Not to Tell," by L. D. Boshes INT SURG 54:
12-16, December, 1970.

"To Tell or Not to Tell," by MacGillis NURS SCI 2:444+,
December, 1964.

"Toledo Team Runs Survey on 'Telling the Patient'," OH
STATE MED J 68:456, May, 1972.

"Values Destroyed by Death," by J. C. Diggory, et al.
J ABNORM SOC PSYCH 63:205-210, July, 1961.

"What Are You and Your Patient Really Saying to Each
Other?" by L. J. Roose MED INSIGHT 3:24-25, February,
1971.

"What Can You Say?" by M. Connor NZ NURS J 66:7, July,
1973.

"What Can You Say to the Cancer Patient?" by V. Barckley NURS OUTLK 6:316-318, June, 1958.

"What I Say When I Have to Give a Prognosis," by M. M.
Ravitch RED PHYS 15:45-47, June, 1969.

"What Philadelphia Physicians Tell Patients with Cancer,"
by W. T. Fitts JAMA 153:901-904, November 7, 1953.

"What Shall We Tell the Cancer Patient?" by J. Marmor
BULL LA CO MED ASS 84:1324,1341-1342, November, 1954.

"What Shall We Tell the Cancer Patient?" by E. Litin,
et al. PROC STAFF MEET MAYO CLIN 35:10, 1960.

"What Should the Surgeon Tell the Cancer Patient?" by
L. D. Leffall, Jr. URBAN HEALTH 1:30-31, June, 1972.

"What to Say to the Cancer Suspect," by S. Wolf CURR
MED DIG 20,4:97-98, April, 1953.

"What to Tell a Child," TIME 67, March 14, 1969.

"What to Tell Cancer Patients," by D. Oken JAMA 175,13:
1120-1128, April 1, 1961.

"What to Tell the Parents of a Child with Cancer," by
R. S. Lourie CLIN PROC CHILD HOSP 17,4:91-99, April,
1961.

"When a Loved One Is Dying ... How to Decide What to
Tell Him," by J. W. Hoffman TODAYS HEALTH 50:40-43,
February, 1972.

"When Cancer is Diagnosed," by Brauer MED INSIGHT 2:20+,
June, 1970.

"When Patients Ask Tough Questions," by G. Oppenheim
MED ECON 38:54-58, January 2, 1961.

"When You Have to Break the Bad News," PHYS MAN 1:56-62,
June, 1961.

"When Your Patient Asks: Do I Have Cancer?" by I. Wolff
RN 23:51-52, May, 1960.

EXECUTION
"The Deterrent Influence of the Death Penalty,"
by K. F. Schuessler ANNALS OF AM ACAD OF POL & SOC
SCI 284:54-62, 1952.

"More Than One Execution: Who Goes First?" by D.
Lester, et al. JAMA 217:215, July 12, 1971.

"Reaction to Extreme Stress: Impending Death by
Execution," by H. Bluestone, et al. AM J PSYCHIAT
119:393-396, November, 1962.

"Stay of Execution: Excerpts," by S. Alsop SAT R
WORLD 1:20-23, December 18, 1973.

"Assisting the Family in Time of Grief," by W. N. Beachy JAMA 202:559-560, November 6, 1967.

"Care of the Dying. Relatives, Professional Care, and the Dying Patient," by E. Wilkes NURS MIRROR 139: 53-56, October 10, 1974.

"The Care of the Dying Patient and His Family," AUST NURS J 2:6, February, 1973.

"Care of the Family of the Child with Cancer," by S. Friedman PEDIAT 40,3:498-507, September, 1967.

"Day Grandad Dies," by A. Bullock PARENTS MAG 28:40-41+, May, 1953.

"A Day with Papa, " by Britton TODAYS HLTH 44:30+, February, 1966.

"Dealing with Death and Dying Through Family-Centered Care, " by K. I. Fond NURS CLIN N AM 7:53-64, March, 1972.

"Dealing with the Grieving Family," by R. A. Kalish RN 26:80-84, May, 1963.

"Death and Nursing. II Patient's Family," by H. Kawano JAP J NURS 37:1481-1489, November, 1973.

"A Death in the Family: a Lay View," by S. Hancock BRIT MED J 1:29-30, January 6, 1973.

"A Death in the Family: A Professional View," by W. F. Anderson BRIT MED J 1:-1-32, January 6, 1973.

"A Death in the Family" a Professional View," by C. Saunders BRIT MED J 1:30-31, January 6, 1973.

"Death Is a Family Matter," by L. Wilkinson RN 33:50-51, September, 1970.

"Development of an Interdisciplinary Team to Care for Dying Patients and Their Families," by F. S. Wald ANA REG CLIN CONF 47-55, 1969.

"Do We Ignore the Grieving Relative?" by A. Pentinmaki
SAIRAANHOITAJA 50:12-15, July 9, 1974.

"Domicillary Care of the Terminally Ill and Their Relatives," by W. Mitchell MIDWIFE HEALTH VISIT 9:366-
367, November, 1973.

"The Dying Patient and His Family," by P. F. Regan JAMA
192:666-667, May 24, 1965.

"The Dying Patient and His Family," by Stitt EMERG MED
2:112+, May, 1970.

"The Dying Patient and His Relatives," by W. Robinson
NURS TIMES 69:651, May 17, 1973.

"Dying Patients and Their Families: How Staff Can Give
Support," by C. R. Kneisl HOSP TOPICS 45:37-39, November, 1967.

"Emotional Management of Family Stressed in Care of Dying Child," by D. A. Howell PEDIAT CURR 17:6, June,
1968.

"Emotions Expressed in Mrs. Takako Takahashi's Nursing
Diary on Her Dying Husband," by C. Bessho COMPR NURS
Q 6:31-36, Spring, 1971.

"Family and Staff During Last Weeks and Days of Terminal
Illness," by A. Strauss ANN NY ACAD SCI 164:687-695,
December 19, 1969.

"Family and the Dying Patient," by H. E. Dunlop GERIAT
NURS 3:15-17, June, 1967.

"Family Tasks and Reactions in the Crisis of Death," by
S. B. Goldberg NURS DIG 2:21-26, May, 1974.

"Family Tasks and Reactions in the Crisis of Death," by
S. B. Goldberg SOC CASEWORK 54:398-405, July, 1973.

"Fatherless Family," by J. L. Despert CHILD STUDY 34,
No.3:22-28, Summer, 1957.

"Film: 'Part of the Family,' on Impact of Death on Family," THE NEW YORK TIMES 95:3, May 19, 1971.

"First Heartbreak," by C. J. Foster PARENTS MAG 29:38-39+, May, 1974.

"I Was My Father's Nurse," by Chura AJN 68:1908+, September, 1968.

"Integrated Family Oriented Cancer Care Program: the Report of a Pilot Project in the Socio-Emotional Management of Chronic Disease," by A. Sheldon, et al., J CHRON DIS 22:743-755, April, 1970.

"The Management of Parents of Acutely Ill Children in the Hospital," by M. Lewis AM J ORTHO 32:60-66, 1962.

"Maternal Age and Parental Loss," by K. L. Grossman BRIT J PSYCHIAT 114:242-243, February, 1968.

"Maternal Age and Parental Loss," by P. A. Moran BRIT J PSYCHIAT 114:207-214, February, 1968.

"The Nurse's Role in Assisting Families of Dying Geriatric Patients to Manage Grief and Guilt," by Schwab ANA CLIN SESS 110+, 1968.

"The Physician's Role Regarding Dying Patients and Their Relatives," by Monnerot-Dumaine PRESSE MED 77:1629-1630, October 25, 1969.

"Prevention of Depression in Relatives of Terminal Patients," by G. Sarmousakis DEL MED J 38:315-317, October, 1966.

"Psychological Impact of Long Illness and Death of a Child on the Family Circle," by B. Cobb J PEDIAT 49,6: 746-751, October-December, 1956.

"Relatives, Professional Care, and the Dying Patient," by E. Wilkes NURS MIRROR 139:53-56, October 10, 1974.

"Should Husband Conceal Her Impending Death From Wife," by A. Bryant ILL LON NEWS 235:430, October 17, 1959.

"Should You Care for a Relative with a Terminal Illness?" by Legge RN 24:77+, September, 1961.

"Some Observations on Death and a Family," by Adamek NURS SCI 3:258+, August, 1965.

"A Study of the Emotional Reactions of Children and Families to Hospitalization and Illness," by D. G. Prugh, et al. AM J ORTHO 23, 1:70-106, January, 1953.

"Terminal Patient and His Family," by H. K. Branson BED NURS 3:21-23, June, 1970.

"Thoughts on the Death of My Father," by R. A. Aurthur ESQUIRE 79:115+, March, 1973.

"We Faced Death," by F. T. Kirkwood PARENTS MAG 26:173, September, 1951.

"When a Loved One Is Dying," by J. W. Hoffman TODAYS HEALTH 50:40-43, February, 1972.

"A Young Boy's Reaction to the Death of His Sister," by B. Rosenblatt J AM ACAD CHILD PSYCHIAT 8:321-325, April, 1969.

FAMILY: HELPING
"Help for the Family Before and After a Death," PT CARE 4:59+, May 31, 1970.

"Helping the Dying Patient and His Family," by C. W. Wahl J PASTOR CARE 26:93-98, June, 1972.

"Helping the Family Face an Impending Death," by O. R. Prattes NURS '73 3:16-20, February, 1973.

"Helping the Patient and the Family Deal with a Crisis Situation," by R. Mazzola, et al. J NEUROSURG NURS 6: 85-88, December, 1974.

"The Management of the Family in Fatal Illness," by E. Wilkes QUEEN'S NURS J 16:150-151, October, 1973.

"Not by Magic: How Can Broken Families Find Healing and Strength?" by F. J. Williams INT J REL ED 43:14-15+, May, 1967.

GERIATRICS: ANXIETY
  SEE ATTITUDES TOWARD DEATH: ANXIETY

GERIATRICS: ATTITUDE TOWARDS DEATH
  SEE ATTITUDES TOWARD DEATH: GERIATRICS

GERIATRICS: CARE
  SEE CARE: GERIATRICS

GERIATRICS: FAMILY
  SEE ALSO FAMILY
  "Emotional Problems of the Geriatric Patient and His Family," by J. Woods SC NURS 22:169-170, Fall, 1970.

  "Grief Work in the Aged Patient," by Burnside NURS FORUM 8:416+, #4, 1969.

  "The Nurse's Role in Assisting Families of Dying Geriatric Patients to Manage Grief and Guilt," by M. L. Schwab ANA CLIN SESS 110-116, 1968.

GERIATRICS: GENERAL
  "Aged and the Dying Process: the Inevitable Decisions," by R. A. Kalish J SOC ISSUES 21: 87-96, October, 1965.

  "The Art of Aging and Dying," by J. W. Eaton GERONTOL 4: 94-100, June, 1964.

  "Contribution to the Study of Senile Maladjustment. II The Attitude Toward Death Examined in a Group of Old People," by A. M. Maderna, et al. J GERONT 11:1009-1016, October, 1963.

  "Death as a Research Problem in Social Gerontology: An Overview," by R. Kastenbaum GERONTOL 6:67-69, June, 1966.

  "Death at Sunset," by M. B. Martin NAT R 26:1356+, November 22, 1974.

  "Death in Sun City," by C. Davis ESQUIRE 66:134-137, October, 1966.

  "Decision Making in the Death Process of the Ill Aged," by M. B. Miller GERIAT 26:105-116, May, 1971.

"Distance from Death as a Variable in the Study of Aging," by M. A. Leiberman, et al. DEV PSYCH 2:(1), 71-84, 1970.

"The Dying Patient," by W. Tarnower GP 40:97-102, July, 1969.

"The Elderly at the End of Life," by W. F. Anderson NURS TIMES 69:193-194, February 8, 1973.

"The End of Life in the Elderly," by R. H. Williams POST-GRAD MED 54:55-59, December, 1973.

"Grief Reactions in Later Life," by K. Stern, et al. AM J PSYCHIAT 58:289-294, 1951.

"The Mental Life of Dying Geriatric Patients," by R. Kast-enbaum GERONTOL 7:97-100, June, 1967.

"Multiple Perspectives on a Geriatric 'Death Valley," by R. Kastenbaum COMMUN MENT H J 3:21-29, Spring, 1967.

"Old Age," by J. Harley NURS TIMES 60:1401-1402, October 23, 1964.

"Old Age and the Fear of Death," by D. Kotsovsky SCHWEIZ Z PSYCHOL 10:42-53, 1951.

"On Being Old and on Dying," by E. C. Kast J AM GERIAT SOC 20:524-530, November, 1972.

"Preparation for Death in Old Age," by A. Lipman, et al. J GERONT 21:426-431, July, 1966.

"Problem of Death and Dying in the Geriatric Patient," by K. Wolff J AM GERIAT SOC 18:954-961, December, 1970.

"Reflections of Aging and Death," by R. Platt LANCET 1: 1-6, January 5, 1963.

"The Significance of Social Psychological Factors for the Death Risk, Especially in Aged Persons," by B. Ekblom NORD PSYKIAT T 18:272-281, 1964.

GERIATRICS: GENERAL

"A Therapeutic Approach to Aging and Dying," by C. E. Preston POSTGRAD MED 54:64-68, December, 1973.

"Treatment of the 'Irremediable" Elderly Patient," by B. Isaacs BRIT MED J 3:526-528, September 8, 1973.

GERIATRICS: NURSING CARE
"Basic Knowledge for Work with Aging," by N. Brill GERONTOL 9:(3), 197-203, 1969.

"The Dying Patient," by Kramer, et al. GERIAT NURS 2: 15+, September-October, 1966.

"The Nurse's Role in Assisting Families of Dying Geriatric Patients to Manage Guilt and Grief," by Schwab ANA CLIN SESSIONS 110+, 1968.

GERIATRICS: NURSING HOME
"Dr. Shrut Reports Study of Group of Aged Living in Institutions Shows Those in Environment Similar to Their Homes Least Preoccupied with Death," THE NEW YORK TIMES 15:1, September 1, 1956.

"Dying: the Career of the Nursing Home Patient," by E. Gustafson J HEALTH SOC BEHAV 13:226-235, September, 1972.

"Relationship of Mortality Rates to Entrance to a Home for the Aged," by M. A. Lieberman GERIAT 16:515-519, 1961.

GERIATRICS: OTHER CULTURES
"The Kuna Indians: Their Attitudes Toward the Aged," by R. L. Wolk, et al. J AM GERIAT SOC 19:406-416, May, 1971.

GERIATRICS: PROBLEMS
"Sociopsychologic Studies of the Aging Process. Problems of Death and the Dying Patient," by A. L. Strauss PSYCHIAT RES REP AM PSYCHIAT ASS 23:198-206, February, 1968.

GERIATRICS: STAFF
"Geriatric Staff Attitudes Toward Death," by D. S. Kazzaz, et al. J AM GERIAT SOC 16:1364-1371, December, 1968.

GERIATRICS: STAFF

"Helping the Geriatric Staff Face Conflicts About Death,"
FRONTIERS OF HOSP PSYCHIAT (ROCHE REPT) 5,20:1-2, 11,
December 1, 1968.

GERIATRICS: TERMINAL ILLNESS
"Old Age, Disease and Death," by T. Geill EXCERPTA MED
3,20:447-450, September, 1960.

"Some Terminal Aspects of Disease in Old Age: A Clinical
Study of 300 Patients," by T. H. Howell J AM GERIAT
SOC 17:1034-1038, November, 1969.

"Terminal Illness in the Aged," by A. N. Exton-Smith
LANCET 2: 305-308, 1961.

GERIATRICS: TIME
"On the Meaning of Time in Later Life," by R. Kastenbaum
J GENETIC PSYCHOL 109:9-25, 1966.

"Views of the Aged on the Timing of Death," by C . E.
Preston, et al. GERONTOL 11:300-304, Winter, 1971.

GERIATRICS: VIEWPOINT
SEE ALSO: ATTITUDES TOWARD DEATH: GERIATRICS
"The Art of Aging and Dying," by J. W. Eaton GERONTOL
4:94-100, June, 1964.

"Attitudes Toward Death (An Interview)," by R. N.
Butler GERIAT 19,2:58A, 62A, 64A, February, 1964.

"Note on the Psychopathology of Senility: Senescent
Defense Against Threat of Death," by R. F. Morgan
PSYCHOL REP 16:305-306, February, 1965.

"Premature Death and Self-Injurious Behavior in Old Age,"
by R. Kastenbaum, et al. GERIAT 26:71-81, July, 1971.

"Sociopsychologic Studies of the Aging Process. Problems
of Death and the Dying Patient," by A. L. Strauss PSY-
CHIAT RES REP AM PSYCHIAT 23:198-206, February, 1968.

GRIEF
SEE BEREAVEMENT

HEART DISEASE
  SEE ATTITUDES TOWARD DEATH: CORONARY CARE PATIENTS

HELP
  SEE CARE

HOME: DYING AT (CANCER PATIENTS)
  "Caring for the Cancer Patient at Home," by V. Barckley
  J PRACT NURS 24:24-27, October, 1974.

  "Domiciliary Care of the Patient with Cancer," by H.
  McCarrick NURS TIMES 65:729, June 5, 1969.

  "Terminal Cancer at Home," by E. Wilkes LANCET 1:799-
  801, April 10, 1965.

  "Terminal Cancer Nursed at Home," by Edwards NM 121:717+,
  March 25, 1966.

  "Terminal Cancer Patients," by M. Pfeiffer, et al. AM J
  PUB HEALTH 43:909-914, 1953.

HOME: DYING AT (CHILDREN)
  "The Child's Request to Die at Home," by G. Davoli PED-
  IAT 38:925, November, 1966.

  "Let the Parents Help Care for the Child with Leukemia,"
  by C. Isler RN 25:44-57, June, 1962.

HOME: HOW TO GIVE CARE
  "At Home with Death," NEWSWEEK 85:43-44, January 6, 1975.

  "Care of the Dying in Their Own Home," by O. Keywood
  NURS TIMES 70:1516-1517, September 26, 1974.

  "Caring for the Terminal Patient in Her Home," by B.
  Shillinglaw AUST NURS J 2:24-25, June, 1973.

  "Dealing with Death and Dying Through Family-Centered
  Care," by K. I. Fond NURS CLIN N AM 7:53-64, March,
  1972.

  "A Death at Home," by D. McNeil CAN NURSE 70:17-19,
  March, 1974.

HOME: HOW TO GIVE CARE

"Domiciliary Care of the Terminally Ill and Their Relatives," by W. Mitchell MIDWIFE HEALTH VISIT 9:366-367, November, 1973.

"Home Care of Terminal Malignant Disease," by R. Gibson J R COLL PHYS LOND 5:135-139, January, 1971.

"Home As the Place to Die," J MED SOC N J 64:640, August, 1972.

"How to Provide Effective Home Care for the Terminally Ill," by E. Wilkes GERIAT 28:93-96, August, 1973.

"Malignant Disease in the Home," by Wilson NURS TIMES 63:1607+, December 1, 1967.

"Supporting the Patient in the Home," by R. Gibson BRIT MED J 1:35-36, January 6, 1973.

"Terminal Illness at Home," by L. W. Batten NURS MIRROR 130:28-31. February 27, 1970.

"To Die at Home," by L. J. Blewett AM J NURS 70:2602-2604, december, 1970.

"Where to Die," by D. Smithers BRIT MED J 1:34-35, January 6, 1973.

HOME: INDIVIDUAL DEATH
"Sarah Wanted to Die at Home -- But Her Family Resisted," by V. Chura NURS '74, 4:16-18, July, 1974.

HOME: OTHER CULTURES AND DEATH
"Terminal Care at Home in Two Cultures," by J. French, et al. AM J NURS 73:502-505, March, 1973.

HOME: PROBLEMS IN DEATH AT
"Domiciliary Care of the Dying -- Some Problems Encountered," by B. J. McNulty NURS MIRROR 136:29-30, May 18, 1973.

"Malignant Disease, Social and Medical Factors Associated with Dying at Home or in the Hospital," by A.W. M. Ward SOC SC MED 8:413-420, July, 1974.

"Problems of the Family with Illness. Cases with Death Occurring at Home," by M. Nishino, et al. JAP J PUBL HEALTH NURS 25:38-46, March, 1969.

HOSPICE

"At St. Christopher's Hospice," by V. Moreton PHYSIOTHERAP 55:68, February, 1969.

"Calvary Hospital, Bronx, Is Only Hospital in NYS Devoted Exclusively to Care of Terminally Ill," THE NEW YORK TIMES 45:1, May 3, 1973.

"Care of Patients Suffering from Terminal Illness at St. Joseph's Hospice, Hackney, London," NM 117:vii, February 14, 1964.

"Caring for the Terminally Ill: A Hospice," by M. D. Kerstein AM J PSYCHIAT 129:237-238, August, 1972.

"Christmas at St. Christopher's," Am J NURS 71:2325-2327, December, 1971.

"Field in Sheffield: St. Luke's Nursing Home for Terminal and Convalescent Patients," NURS TIMES 65:687, May 29, 1969.

"Filling the Gap Between Home and Hospital: St. Ann's Hospice, England," NURS MIRROR 134:17, February 4, 1972.

"For the Terminally Ill: A Hospital That Cares(London, England St. Christopher's Hospice) MED WORLD NEWS 15:46-47, July 19, 1974.

"Good Death at St. Christopher's Hospice," by C. N. Barnard FAM HEALTH 5:40+, April, 1973.

"Havens of Peace," by P. A. Downie NURS TIMES 69:1068-1070, August 16, 1973.

"Hospice for the Dying Planned in Greater New Haven," HOSP MANAG 112:19, August, 1971.

"Hostel of God," NURS MIRROR 139:66-68, October 10, 1974.

"New Haven Hospice Provides Home Care for Terminally Ill," AM J NURS 74:717, April, 1974.

"Relief of Pain: Prerequisite to the Care and Comfort of the Dying ... St. Christopher's Hospice in London, England," by E. Janzen NURS FORUM 13:48-51, #1, 1974.

"St. Christopher's Hospice," by Weist INT NURS REV 14: 38, September-October, 1967.

"St. Christopher's Hospice in London Described," MED WORLD NEWS 15:46-47, July 19, 1974.

"St. Christopher's Hospice... Sydenham, England," by T. Ingles NURS OUTLK 22:759-763, December, 1974.

"St. Christopher's Outpatients," by B. J. McNulty AM J NURS 71:2328-2330, December, 1971.

"Talk or Terminal Care? Connecticut's Hospice, Inc.," by E. F. Dobihal, Jr. CONN MED 38:364-367, July, 1974.

"Terminal Care: Connecticut Corporation Will Build a Hospital for the Dying," MOD HEALTHCARE, SHORT TERM CARE ED 2:101+, July, 1974.

"A Visit to St. Christopher's Hospital in London," by J. Schouten NEDERL T GENEESK 112:704-706, April 13, 1968.

"Yale Plans 'Hospice' Like St. Christopher's," AM J NURS 71:2296, December, 1971.

HOSPITAL

"The Care of the Dying-- Whose Job Is It?" by E. Kubler-Ross PSYCHIAT MED 1:103-107, April, 1970.

"Community of Care," by P. J. Lee NC MED J 35:96-98, February, 1974.

"Death, Dying and the Neurosurgical Service," by J. Ransohoff J NEUROSURG NURS 5:2-6, July, 1973.

"Death in the Hospital: A Problem for Study," by S. P. Spitzer, et al. NURS FORUM 3:85-92, #4, 1964.

"Dying on Time. Arranging the Final Hours of Life in a Hospital," by Glaser, et al. HOSP TOPICS 43:28+, August, 1965.

"The Dying Patient -- A Team Affair," by A. Barrocas NURS DIG 2:62-66, May, 1974.

"The Hospital and the Dying Patient," by D. F. Philipps HOSP 46:68+, February 16, 1972.

"Hospital Care of the Dying," by J. M. Holford J SOC SERV REV 82:2804, December 16, 1972.

"Hospital Unit for Dying Patients," by Krant HOSP PRACT 7:101-108, January, 1972.

"Institutional Care of the Terminally Ill," by Z. M. Cotter HOSP PROG 52:42-48, June, 1971.

"Improved Care in Hospitals," by Phillips HOSP 46:68-75, February 16, 1972.

"Medical Management of Incurably Sick Patients and Patients in Terminal Stages of Disease and Modern Therapeutic Possibilities Available in Hospitals," by A. Wozna POL TYG LEK 26:1955-1957, December 13, 1971.

"Most Deaths Now Occur in Hospitals," STATIS BULL MET LIFE INS CO 41:6-8, November, 1960.

"The Non-Accountability of Terminal Care," by A. L. Strauss, et al. HOSP 38:73-87, 1964.

"The Plight of Dying Patients in Hospitals," by F. Mervyn AM J NURS 71:1988-1990, October, 1971.

"Primary Task of the Hospital," by M. Wilson HOSP 66: 346-349, October, 1970.

"The Social Ecology of Dying: Observations of Wards for the Terminally Ill," by D. K. Reynolds, et al. HOSP COMM PSYCHIAT 25:147-152, March, 1974.

HOSPITAL

"Terminal Care Units," by E. Wilkes J COLL GEN PRACT 12:
313-318, November, 1966.

"Thanatophobia in Hospitalized Patients," by M. Bialowas
WIAD LEK 27:395-396, February 15, 1974.

"We Have No Dying Patients," by L. Robinson NURS OUTLK
22:651-653, October, 1974.

"Where to Die," by D. Smithers BRIT MED J 1:34-35, January 6, 1973.

HOSPITAL: CHILDREN WHO ARE DYING
"On a Teaching Hospital's Responsibility to Counsel
Parents Concerning Their Child's Death," by H. Williams
MED J AUST 2, 16:633-645, October, 1963.

"Practice of Pediatrics: Participation of Parents in the
Hospital Care of Fatally Ill Children," by A. G. Knud-
son PEDIAT 26,3:482-490, September, 1960.

HOSPITAL: DISCHARGE
"Discharge of the Terminally Ill Patient," by B. McNulty
NURS TIMES 66:1160-1162, September 10, 1970.

HOSPITAL: GARRISON HOSPITAL
"Organization of the Treatment of Patients with Trauma-
tic Shock and in Términal State in Garrison Hospitals,"
by B. L. Meerovich VOENNOMED ZH 11:56-57, November,
1965.

HOSPITAL: STAFF INTERACTION
"Role Perception in Hospital Interaction," by K. I.
Kogan, et al. NURS RES 10,2:75-78, Spring, 1961.

"Some Possible Consequences of Limited Communication
Between Patients and Hospital Functionaries," by J.
Skipper, et al. J HEALTH HUM BEHAV 5,1:34-39, 1964.

HOSTILITY
SEE ATTITUDES TOWARD DEATH: GENERAL

HUMOR
SEE DEATH: HUMOR

"An Impressive Death," by H. Tomita KANGO 24:14-18, September, 1972.

"Birthday in Heaven," by M. R. Patricia CATH SCHL J 64: 65+, February, 1964.

"Carl and Willy," by Miles NURS FORUM 8:146+, #2, 1969.

"Dear Carl," by S. Van Dyke IMPRINT 20:20+, December, 1973.

"Death as an Event: A Commentary on Robert Morison," by L. R. Kass SCIENCE 173:698-702, August 20, 1971.

"Death Enlightened. A Study of Frederik Ruysch," by A. M. Luyendijk-Eishout JAMA 212:121-126, April 6, 1970.

"Death of a Neighbor," by M. E. Human AM J NURS 73:1914-1916, November, 1973.

"The Death of Mozart," by A. S. MacNalty NURS MIRROR 124:8-10, June 16, 1967.

"Declaration of Sydney -- A Statement on Death," J IRISH MED ASS 61:406, November, 1968.

"Eli," by M. Oerlemans AM J NURS 72:14401441, August, 1972.

"Farewell to a Friend," by McDonald AM J NURS 68:773, April, 1968.

"Feather of a Dove; A Husband's Tribute to His Wife:Excerpt from More Than Booty," by B. Crile REDBOOK 126: 42-43+, January, 1966.

"Going of Him," by W. Connor NEW STATESMAN 69:877, June 4, 1965.

"Home for Christmas," by S. Leighton AMERICA 106:421-422, December 23, 1961.

"I Promise You, It Will Be All Right; Dilemma of a Friend's Dying," by J. Barthel LIFE 72:55-56+, March 17, 1972.

"I'll Go On Working After Death," by M. Alson MCCALLS 80:22, May, 1953.

"In Memory of Mike," by D. J. Blackmore CORONET 47:52-56, January, 1960.

"JH," by D. Warzyn BEDSIDE NURS 4:29-30, August, 1971.

"Jeanette: No Hope for Cure," by E. G. Nichols NURS FORUM 11:97-104, 1972.

"Johnny, the Little Boy Who Never Smiles," by D. White-house AM J NURS 55, 9:1110, September, 1955.

"Laura Was Unpleasant and Made Us Angry. But She Was Dying. And That Made Us Ashamed," by P. Reilly NURS '73 3:44-46, August, 1973.

"Lesson in Bravery: Reflections on the Kennedy Children's Ordeal After Their Father Was Shot," by G. Caplan, et al. MCCALLS 95:85+, September, 1968.

"Light of a Nun's Death," by D. Grumpach CATH WORLD 194:236-241, January, 1962.

"Margaret: A Study in Perception," by S. Macmillan NURS TIMES 68:1644-1646, December 28, 1972.

"Michael," by V. Coleman NURS TIMES 69:213, February 15, 1973.

"Molly," by S. Zator RN 34:50-52+, November, 1971.

"Mr. C.," by S. Legendre BEDSIDE NURSE 5:21-22, May, 1972.

"My Husband Crashed in the Jungle," E. Bowne SAT EVE POST 227:36-37+, April 30, 1955.

"My Last Wonderful Days," by H. B. Andre FARM J 80:31-31+, July, 1956; Same abridged as "My Last Best Days on Earth," READ DIG 69:73-76, October, 1956.

"The Night Nell Died," by J. S. Hays NURS OUTLK 10:801-803, December, 1962.

INDIVIDUAL: DEATH OF AN

"Paul, the Silent Teacher," by S. Nau, et al. INFIRM CAN 61:712-716, November, 1965

"Peter and Annette," NURS TIMES 69:243, February 22, 1973.

"Randy, the Silent Teacher," by S. Nau, et al. CAN NURS 61:903-906, November, 1965.

"Rest in Peace, Ruthless Roger," by P. B. Eisenberg AM J NURS 70:132, January, 1970.

"Sarah Wanted to Die at Home -- But Her Family Resisted," by V. Chura NURS '74 4:16-18, July, 1974.

"Stephens," BULL AM PROT HOSP ASS 37:65-70,#2, 1973.

"They Cheated Death," by I. Leiberman AM MERC 85:82-85, July, 1957.

"Vinnie Was Dying. But He Wasn't the Problem. I Was," by E. B. Marino NURS '74 4:46-47, February, 1974.

"We Called Her Job," by Lovelace PN 20:42+, June, 1970.

"Who Cared About Tony?" by K. M. Poi AM J NURS 72:1848-1851, October, 1972.

"Why Did Joe Die?" by R. Eisman AM J NURS 71:501-503, March, 1971.

"Willie's Drunk and Nellie's Dying; There Ain't Nobody Free," by C. Kurtagh NURS FORUM 11:221-225, #2, 1972. Also in MICH NURS 44:8, July, 1971.

MARANTOLOGY
SEE ALSO: EDUCATION
"And Now Marantology?" J MED SOC NJ 69:304, April, 1972.

"Dr. Poe Proposes Marantology," THE NEW YORK TIMES 46:1, January 16, 1972.

"Urges New Medical Specialty to Aid Dying: Marantology," CHR CENT 89:163, February 9, 1972.

MOURNING
SEE BEREAVEMENT

"Death and the Dying Patient," by Regan MED INSIGHT 1: 48+, December, 1969.

"Death and the Dying Person," by J. Jollett PERSPECTIVAS 1:37-41, April, 1973.

"The Dying and the Gravely Ill Patient," by C. Lamontagn VIE MED CAN FR 2:517-518, June, 1973.

"Dying Patient," LANCET 2:1238-1239, December 9, 1972.

"The Dying Patient," by J. W. Annis PSYCHOSOM 10:289-292 September-October, 1969.

"The Dying Patient," by O. G. Brim, et al. AM SOC REV 36 1169-1170, December, 1971.

"The Dying Patient," by P. Chodoff MED ANN D C 29:447-450, August, 1960.

"The Dying Patient," by E. G. Dowsett LANCET 2:1416, December 30, 1972.

"The Dying Patient," by P. C. Gibson PRACT 186, 1111:85-91, January, 1961.

"Dying Patient," by S. M. Hamilton J PRACT NURS 21:25, May, 1971.

"The Dying Patient," HAREFUAH 84:336-338, March 15, 1973

"Dying Patient," by A. T. Hunter, et al. CAN MED ASS J 106:369-371, February 19, 1972.

"The Dying Patient," by C. Kram, et al. PSYCHOSOM 10:293-295, September-October, 1969.

"The Dying Patient," by C. H. Kramer GERIAT NURS 2: 15-2 September-October, 1966.

"Dying Patient," by E. L. Maginnis NEB STATE MED J 54: 217-220, April, 1969.

"The Dying Patient," by R. Noyes DIS NERV SYST 28:790-797, December, 1967.

PATIENT: DYING

"The Dying Patient," by T. Rich MIND PSYCHIAT GEN PRACT 1,1:15, 18-19, January, 1963.

"The Dying Patient," by L. J. Roose INT J PSYCHOANAL 50: 385-395, 1969.

"The Dying Patient," by W. C. Scott CAN MED ASS J 106: 1054, May 20, 1972.

"The Dying Patient," by A. D. Weisman FOREST HOSP PUB 1: 16-21, 1962.

"The Dying Patient: A News Awareness -- and a New Dignity," by M. J. Krant TUFTS HEALTH SCI REV 1:32-39, Winter/Spring, 1971.

"Dying Patient Manages Own Medication Plan," AM J NURS 72:627, April, 1972.

"The Dying Patient. When the Focus Must Be Changed," by W. H. Baltzell ARCH INTERN MED 127:106-109, January, 1971.

"Dying Patients," by L. Witzel MED KLIN 68:1373-1375, October 15, 1973.

"Experiences with Dying Patients," AM J NURS 73:1058-1064, June, 1973.

"The Patient with a Fatal Illness," by M. Oelrich AM J OCCUP THERAP 28:429-432, August, 1974.

"Perspectives on Death and the Dying Patient," by F. Webster HOSP PROG 54:32-34, December, 1973.

"The Sickbed of the Incurable Patient," by H. R. Bax NEDERL T GENEESK 100, 3, 36:2601-2610, September, 1956.

PATIENT: FRIEND OF A DYING
"Death of a Neighbor," by M. E. Human AM J NURS 73:1914-1916, November, 1973.

"Farewell to a Friend," by M. McDonald AM J NURS 68:773, April, 1968.

PATIENT: FRIEND OF A DYING

"Test of Friendship," by E. Poehlman RN 34:42-43+, October, 1971.

PATIENT: GRIEF
"The Dying Patient's Grief," by C. K. Aldrich JAMA 184: 329-331, May 4, 1963.

"The Dying Patient's Grief," by L. H. Nahum CONN MED 28: 241-245, April, 1964.

PATIENT: HOSPITAL
"The Dying Patient and the Hospital: An Attitude Sampling," by Kellett HOSP ADMIN 10:26+, Fall, 1965.

PATIENT: NEEDS
"Do You Often Lose Touch with a Dying Patient?" PT CARE 4:18+, May 31, 1970.

"The Dying Patient and His Human Needs," by M. M. Pipp EPHETA 10:4-10, April-June, 1971.

"Focus on the Patient, Not on the Fact of His Dying," PT CARE 4:41+, May 31, 1970.

"Importance of Removing Dying Patients from Loneliness and Isolation," THE NEW YORK TIMES 29:2, January 15, 1973.

"Treatment of a Dying Female Patient," by J. Norton PSYCHE 22:99-117, February, 1968.

PATIENT: POINT OF VIEW
"As the Patient Sees It: Public Dying," by Joan Nelson MED WORLD 80,5: 596-599, May, 1954.

"The Behavior of Dying Patients," by L. Witzel MED KLIN 66:577-578, April 9, 1971.

"Death and Dying: Attitudes of Patient and Doctor," by R. H. Dovenmuhle GROUP ADV PSYCHIAT 5: 607-613, October, 1965.

"Death and Dying: Attitudes of Patient and Doctor, IV," by I. M. Greenberg GROUP ADV PSYCHIAT 5:623-631, October , 1965.

PATIENT: POINT OF VIEW

"Dying -- From the Patient's Point of View," by E.
Kubler-Ross TRIANGLE 13:25-26, 1974.

"How the Patient Faces Death," by E. Kubler-Ross
PUBLIC WELFARE 29:56-60, January, 1971.

"Lessons from a Dying Patient," by D. Sharp AM J NURS
68:1517-1520, July, 1968.

"A Patient's Concern with Death," by J. M. Baker, et al.
AM J NURS 63:90-92, July, 1963.

"The Patient's Point of View," by E. Null OKLA NURS 48:
1, January, 1973.

PATIENT: PROBLEMS
"Problems of Impending Death. The Concerns of the Dy-
ing Patient," by A. W. Reed PHYS THERAP 48:740-743,
July, 1968.

PEDIATRICS
SEE CHILDREN

PERCEPTION
SEE ATTITUDES TOWARD DEATH

PERSONALITY
ALSO SEE PSYCHIATRY
"Personality Factors in Denial of Illness," by E. A.
Weinstein ARCH NEUR PSYCHIAT 69:355-367, 1953.

"Personality and Intellectual Changes in Leukemia: A
Case Study, " by B. I. Murstein J PROJECT TECH 22,4:
421-426, December, 1958.

PHILOSOPHY
"Philosophic Implications of Terminal Illness," by J. A.
Knight N CAR MED J 22:493-495, October, 1961.

"Survivors of Cardiac Arrest," by R. G. Druss, et al.
JAMA 201:291-296, July 31, 1967.

"Values Destroyed by Death," by J. C. Diggory, et al.
J ABNORM SOC PSYCHOL 63, 1:205-210, 1961.

PSYCHIATRIC MANAGEMENT OF DYING PATIENTS
SEE ALSO: CANCER: PSYCHIATRIC ASPECTS
PSYCHOLOGICAL MANAGEMENT OF DYING PATIENTS

"A Psychiatric Approach to the Dying Patient," by P.
Chodoff CA 10:29-32, January-February, 1960.

"Psychiatric Approach to Patients with Malignant
Disease," by C. H. H. Branch ROCKY MOUNT MED J 49:
749-753, 1952.

"Psychiatric Consultation in Fatal Illness," by J. Hinton PROC ROY SOC MED 65:1035-1038, November, 1972.

"A Psychiatric Evaluation of Communicating with the Dying," by F. L. Patry DIS MENT SYST 26:715-718, March,
1965.

"Psychiatric Help for the Incurable Patient," by S.
Cohen THE PHYSICIAN'S PANORAMA 5,8:12-20, October,
1967.

"Psychiatric Intervention in the Case of a Terminally
Ill College Student," by J. McMurrer, et al. J AM COLL
HEALTH ASS 22:134-137, December, 1973.

"Psychiatric Management of Operative Syndromes: 1. The
Therapeutic Consultation and the Effect of Noninter-
pretive Intervention," by T. Hackett, et al. PSYCHO-
SOM MED 22:267-282, 1960.

"Terminal Hypnosis in Lieu of Terminal Hospitalization;
An Effective Alternative in Fortunate Cases," by W. L.
LaBaw GERONT CLIN 11:312-320, 1969.

PSYCHIATRISTS AND DEATH
"The Psychiatrist and the Cancer Patient," by J. D.
Trawick, Jr. DIS NERV SYST 11,9:278-280, September,
1950.

"The Psychiatrist and the Dying Hospital Patient," by
F. F. Wagner MENT HYG 51:486-488, October, 1967.

"The Psychiatrist and the Dying Hospital Patient," by
F. F. Wagner UGESKR LAEG 129:389-390, March 23, 1967.

"Activation of Mourning and Growth by Psychoanalysis,"
by J. Fleming INT J PSYCHOANAL 44:419-431, 1963.

"An Acute Death Threat: Myrocardial Infarct. Its
Psychoanalytic Emphasis in the Light of Kleinian Concepts," by I. Luchina, et al. REV PSICOANAL 19:103-
106, January-June, 1962.

"Adaptation to Open Heart Surgery: A Psychiatric Study
of Response to Threat of Death," by H. S. Abram AM
J PSYCHIAT 122:659-668, December, 1965.

"Affective Response to Psychoanalytic Death Symbols,"
by W. W. Meissner J ABNORM SOC PSYCHOL 56:295-299,
1958.

"Apropos of a Case Report. Reflection on Death and
Paranoia," by J. Carrere, et al. ANN MEDICOPSYCHOL
122:408-410, October, 1964.

"Asthma and the Fear of Death," by K. J. Monsour PSYCHO-
ANAL Q 29:56-71, 1960.

"Asthma, Melancholia, and Death, I. Psychoanalytic Considerations," by P. H. Knapp, et al. PSYCHOSOM MED 28:
114-133, March-April, 1966.

"Asthma, Melancholia, and Death,II. Psychosomatic Considerations," by P. H. Knapp, et al. PSYCHOSOM MED 28:
134-154, March-April, 1966.

"Attitudes Toward Death of Psychiatric Patients,"by P.
Harder INT J NEURO 3:10-14, February, 1967.

"Behavior Modification for Terminally Ill Patients," by
H. H. Whitman, et al. AJN 75:98-101, January, 1975.

"Care of the Dying: Mental Distress in the Dying," by
Saunders NURS TIMES 55:1067+, October 30, 1959.

"Castration Anxiety and the Fear of Death," by I. Sarnoff,
et al. J PERSONAL 27:374-385, 1959.

"Clinical Perspective on Dying," by R. G. Janes CAN MED
ASS J 107:425+, September 9, 1972.

"The Concept of Death in Psychiatry," by M. Komiyama
JAP J NURS 37:624-626, May, 1973.

"Coping with Waiting: Psychiatric Intervention and
Study in the Waiting Room of a Pediatric Oncology
Clinic," by I. Hoffman, et al. COMPR PSYCHIAT 12:
67-81, January, 1971.

"Current Psychotherapeutic Perspectives in the Doctor-
Patient Relationship," by H. G. deAraujo J MED 47:
237-245, February, 1962.

"Curvilinearity Between Dream Con-ent and Death Anxiety
and the Relationship of Death Anxiety to Repression-
Sensitization," by P. J. Handal, et al. J ABNORM
PSYCHOL 77:11-16, February, 1971.

"Death and Confidentiality," by A. D. Bucove AM J PSYCH-
IAT 127:845, December, 1970.

"Death and Dying: A Psychoanalytic Perspective," by G.
Benson, Jr. HOSP PROG 53:52-55, March, 1972.

"Death and Nursing. 9. Clinical Nursing and Death. (2).
Psychosomatic Nursing," by H. Kawano JAP J NURS 37:
1200-1207, September, 1973.

"Death and Responsibility: A Psychiatrist's View," by A.
Weisman PSYCHIAT OP 3:22-26, 1966.

"Death and the Self," by R. L. Fulton J RELIG & HEALTH
3:359-368, 1964.

"Death As a Countertransference," by A. Burton PSYCHOANA
49:3-20, Winter, 1962.

"Death by Cursing -- A Problem for Forensic Psychiatry,"
by A. A. Watson MED SCI LAW 13:192-194, July, 1973.

"The Death Instincts -- A Contribution to the Study of
Instincts," by M. Ostow INT J PSYCHOANAL 39, 1:5-16,
1958.

"Death of a Patient During Psychotherapy," by W. H.
Young PSYCHIAT   23:103-108, 1960.

"Death of the Leader in a Group of Schizophrenics," by
M. P. Dumont INT J GROUP PSYCHOTHERAP 16:209-216, 1966.

"Does Life Flash Back at Threat of Death," by J. Snider
SCI DIG 73:48+, January, 1973.

"Dreams of a Dying Patient," by H. R. Greenberg, et al.
BRIT J MED PSYCHOL 43:355-362, December, 1970.

"The Dying Patient, His Physician and the Psychiatric
Consultant," by W. Hicks, et al. PSYCHOSOM 9:47-52,
January-February, 1968.

"A Dying Patient in a Psychotherapy Group," by H. W. Wylie, Jr., et al. INT J GROUP PSYCHOTHERAP 14:482-490,
October, 1964.

"The Dying Patient: Psychological Needs of the Patient,
His Family, and the Physician," by W. Tarnower NEB MED
J 54:6-10, January, 1969.

"Early Parent Death and Mental Illness," by J. Birtchnell
BRIT J PSYCHIAT 116:281-288, March, 1970.

"Ego Identity and the Fear of Death and Dying," by M.
Grotjahn J HILL HOSP 9,3:147-155, July, 1960.

"Emotional Reactions Associated with Death," by J. Ellard MED J AUST 1:979-983, June 8, 1968.

"Emotional Reactions to the Threat of Impending Death,"
by I. W. Browne, et al. IRISH J MED SCI 6:177-187,
April, 1967.

"An Existential Approach to Death," by R. Assell COMPR
NURS Q 5:36-46, Winter, 1970.

"An Existential Approach to Death," by R. Assell NURS
FORUM 8:200-211, 1969.

"Experience, Hallucinations, and Death Certitude," by H.
Kunz Z KLIN PSYCHOL PSYCHOTHER 20:344-347, 1972.

"Fantasies of Women Confronting Death," by E. Greenberger J CONSULT PSYCHOL 29:252-260, June, 1965.

"Fear of Death and Neurosis," by M. M. Stern J AMER PSY-
CHOANAL ASS 16:3-31, January, 1968.

"The Fear of Death As an Indispensable Factor in Psychotherapy," by H. R. Rosenthal AM J PSYCHOTHERAP 17:619-
630, 1963.

"Finality and Death As a Problem of Psychotherapy," by
W. Schulte WIEN MED WSCHR 112:143-146, February 17,
1962.

"Four Recurring Themes," by K. R. Porter BRIT MED J 1:
40-41, January 6, 1973.

"Freud and Death," TIME 100:33, July 17, 1972.

"The Funeral of a Psychiatric Aide," by R. A. Schmie-
deck BULL MENN CLIN 36:641-645, November, 1972.

"Hypoanalytic Elucidation of the Hypnosis Death Concept,"
by J. M. Schneck PSYCHIAT Q (Suppl.) 24:286-289, 1950.

"I Spoke with the Dead," by E. C. Frankel AJN 69:105-107,
January, 1969.

"Idea of Death in Existentialism," by J. G. Gray J PHILOS
48:113-127, March 1, 1951.

"The Impact of Death of a Leader on a Group Process," by
M. Aronson, et al. AM J PSYCHOTHERAP 16, 3:460-468,
July, 1962.

"Inconsistency in the Fear of Death of Individuals," by
D. Lester PSYCHOL REP 20:Suppl 1084, June, 1967.

"Induction of Psychological Death in Rhesus Monkeys," by
H. F. Reslow, et al. J AUTISM CHILD SCHIZO 3:299-307,
October-December, 1973.

"Jung's Sermons to the Dead," by N. Fodor PSYCHOANAL REV
51:74-78, Spring, 1964.

"Kneller, Heidegger, and Death," by D. Vandenberg ED THEORY 15:217-221+, July, 1965.

"Kneller, Heidegger, and Death,D Vandenberg; A Reply," by A. E. DeSoto ED THEORY 16:239-241, July, 1966.

"Letter:'Dying with their Psychiatric Rights on," by H. M. Silverberg AM J PSYCHIAT 131:725, June, 1974.

"Listening to Whisperings. Observations on Living and Dying of Severely Retarded Persons, " by G. Vandermost TI JDSCHR ZIE KENVERPL 27:662-667, July 16,1974.

"Managing the Emotional Problems of the Cancer Patient," by J. Finesinger, et al. CA BULL CANCER PROG 3:19-31, January, 1953.

"Mental Care of Hopeless Patients," SYGEPLEJERSKEN 72: 3, July 27, 1972.

"Misgivings and Misconceptions in the Psychiatric Care of Terminal Patients," by A. D. Weisman PSYCHIAT 33: 67-81, February, 1970.

"Normality, Mask of Death," by J. Chambon REV FR PSYCH-ANAL 36:421-425, May, 1972.

"Note on the Psychopathology of Senility: Senescent Defense Against Threat of Death," by R. F. Morgan PSYCHOL REP 16:305-306, February, 1965.

"The Older Depressed Patient," by W. C. Alvarez GERIAT 28:162, November, 1973.

"On Death, Psychoanalytic Notes on a Basic Fantasy," by M. Abadi REV PSICOANAL 17:431-448, October-December, 1960.

"On Death and Death Symbolism: The Hiroshima Disaster," by R. J. Lifton PSYCHIAT 27:191-210, August, 1964.

"On the Origin of Death. A Psychoanalytic and Ethnological Study on the Fear of Death," by W. Muensterberger PSYCHE 17:169-184, June, 1963.

"Parent Death in Relation to Age and Parental Age at Birth in Psychiatric Patients and General Population Controls," by J. Birtchnell BRIT J PREV SOC MED 23: 244-250, November, 1969.

"A Pathologist's Experience with Attitudes Toward Death," by A. A. Angrist R I MED J 43, 11:693-697, November, 1960.

"The Patient with Inoperable Cancer from the Psychiatric and Social Standpoints," by B. Gerle, et al. CANCER 13, 6: 1206-1217, 1960.

"Perception of Death," by H. Feifel ANN NY ACAD SCI 164: 669-677, December 19, 1969.

"The Perception of Death," by J. R. Folta NURS RES 14: 232-235, Summer, 1965.

"Personality Factors in Denial of Illness," by E. A. Weinstein ARCH NEUR PSYCHIAT 69:355-367, 1953.

"Personality and Intellectual Changes in Leukemia: A Case Study," by B. I. Murstein J PROJECT TECH 22,4: 421-426, December, 1958.

"Phallic Fantasies, Fear of Death and Ecstacy," by S. Pederson AM IMAGO 17, 1"21-46, 1960.

"Psychogenic Death," by G. V. Barrett, et al. SCIENCE 167:(3916), 304-306, 1970.

"Psychological Aspects of Management of Children with Malignant Diseases," by J. B. Richmond, et al. AMER J DIS CHILD 1,89:42-47, 1955.

"Psychological Reactions of Hospitalized Male Patients to a Heart Attack: Age and Social-Class Differences," by J. Rosen, et al. PSYCHOSOM MED 28:808-821, 1966.

"The Role of the Psychiatrist in a General Hospital," by R. M. Kaufman PSYCHIAT Q 27:367-381, 1953.

"Treatment of a Dying Patient," by J. Norton PSYCHOANAL STUD CHILD 18:541-560, 1963.

PSYCHIATRY AND DEATH: TEACHING ABOUT
"Psychiatric Consultation with Nurses on a Leukemia Service," by Wodinsky MENT HYG 48:282+, April, 1964.

"Seminar Using Preventive and Social Psychiatry to Aid Young Physicians Who Must Care for Terminal Patients," by Artiss, et al. N ENG J MED 288:1210-1214, June 7, 1973.

"Teaching Psychiatry in the Context of Dying and Death," by D. Barton AM J PSYCHIAT 130:1290-1291, November, 1973.

"Trauma, Mortal Fear and Fear of Death in Psychoanalytic Theory and Practice," by M. M. Stern PSYCHE 26:901-928, December, 1972.

PSYCHOLOGICAL MANAGEMENT OF DYING PATIENTS
SEE ALSO PSYCHIATRIC MANAGEMENT OF DYING PATIENTS
"The Possibility for Psychological Growth in a Dying Person," by J. Zinker, et al. J GEN PSYCH 74:185-199, 1966.

"Psychological Care of Patients with Terminal Illness," by W. A. Cramond NURS TIMES 69:339-343, March 15, 1973.

"The Psychological Care of P tients with Terminal Illness," by W. A. Cramond NZ NURS J 66:27-29, September, 1972; 66:23-25, October, 1973.

"The Psychological Care of the Cancer Patient," by E. Callaway J MED ASS GEORGIA 41:503-504, November, 1952.

"The Psychological Management of Cancer Patients," by N. S. Kline, et al. JAMA 146, 17:1547-1551, August 25, 1951.

"Psychological Management of the Patient with Incurable Cancer," by B. Murphey GERIAT 8:130-134, 1953.

"The Psychological Needs and Care of the Dying Patient,"
by H. Cooper S AFR MED J 47:1711-1713, September 22,
1973.

"Psychological Problems in Terminal Cancer Management,"
by A. Rothenberg CANCER 14:1063-1073, September-October, 1961.

"A Psychology Program in a Cancer Research Hospital," by
B. R. Cobb, et al. HOSP TX REP BIOL MED 12: 30-38,
1954.

"Three Processes of Dying and Their Behavioral Effects,"
by K. A. Chandler J CONSULT PSYCHOL 29:296-301, August,
1965.

"Transference and Countertransference in the Case of a
Dying Patient," by F. Joseph PSYCHOANAL 49:21-34,
Winter, 1962.

"Understanding Fear Can Bring Comfort," by E. C. Payne,
Jr. CURR MED NEWS 13, July 4-5, 1964.

"Values Destroyed by Death," by J. C. Diggory, et al.
J ABNORM SOC PSYCHOL 63, 1:205-210, 1961.

"'West' as a Symbol of Death," by L. L. Altman PSYCHO-
ANAL Q 28,2: 236-241, April, 1959.

"When Fear Is Healthy," by I. Janis PSYCHOL TODAY 1, 11:
46-49, 60-61, April, 1968.

PSYCHOLOGY OF DEATH
"Predilection to Death. Death and Dying as a Psychiatric
Problem," by A. D. Weisman PSYCHOSOM MED 23:232-256,
May-June, 1961.

"Psychedelic Mystical Experience in the Human Encounter
with Death," by W. N. Pahnke HARV THEOL R 62:1-32,
January, 1969.

"Psychodynamic Formulation of Conflict," by A. D. Weisman ARCH GEN PSYCHIAT 1:288, 1959.

"Psychodynamics of Death," by G. Ammon MED WEIT 15:575-578, April 10, 1971.

"Psychodynamics of the Dying Patient," by T. B. Hagglund DUODECIM 86:10-26, 1970.

"A Psychological Analysis of Discomfort, Pain, and Death," by F. C. Shontz J GEN PSYCHOL 60:275-287, 1959.

"Psychological Aspects of Human Death," by A. Jores MED KLIN 54,7:237-241, February 13, 1959.

"Psychological Autopsy," SCI AM 219:60, October, 1968.

"Psychological Correlates of Impending Death: Some Preliminary Observations," by M. A. Lieberman J GERONT 20:181-190, April, 1965.

"Psychological Factors and Death," by K. A. Achte NORD PSYKIAT T 19:268-273, 1965.

"Psychological Impact of Cancer and Its Treatment. III The Adaptation of Mothers to the Threatened Loss of Their Children Through Leukemia. Part I," by M. Bozeman, et al. CANCER 8,1:1-20, January-February, 1955.

"Psychological Implications of Breathing Difficulties in Poliomyelitis," by M. A. Seidenfeld AM ORTHOP 25,4:788-801, October, 1955.

"Psychological Mechanisms in Patients with Cancer," by H. C. Shands CANCER 4,6:1159-1170, 1951.

"Psychological Reactions in Fatal Illness. I. The Prospect of Impending Death," by A. Verwoerdt J AM GERIAT SOC 15:9-19, January, 1967.

"Psychological Reactions to Impending Death," by Elmore, et al. HOSP TOPICS 45:35+, November, 1967.

"Psychology of Death," NEWSWEEK 76:103-104, September 14, 1970.

"Psychology of a Doomed Family," by D. Langsley AM J Psy-CHOTHERAP 15:531-538, 1961.

"The Psychology of Dying," by D. Cappon PAST   PSYCHOL
12, 111: 35-44, February, 1961.

"The Psychology of Terminal Illness as Portrayed in
Solzhenitsyn's The Cancer Ward," by H. S. Abraham
ARCH INTERN MED 124:758-760, December, 1969.

"Psychopathologic Aspects of a Necrophobia," by W.
Strauss PSYCHIAT NEUROL 154:273-287, 1967.

"The Realm of Death: An Emerging Area of Psychological
Research," by R. Kastenbaum J HUM REL 13:538-552, 1965.

"Regression and Restitution in Object Loss," by A. E.
Scharl PSYCHOANAL STUD CHILD 16:471-480, 1961.

"The Right Way to Die," by A. D. Weisman PSYCHIAT & SOC
SC REV 2:2-7, 1968.

"Significance of the Experience of the Fear of Death,"
by H. Lenz ACT NEUROVEG 4,4-5:534-542, 1952.

"Some Forms of Sympathy: A Phenomenological Analysis,"
by H. Becker J ABNORM SOC PSYCHOL 26:56-68, April,
1951.

"The Survivors of Cardiac Arrest. A Psychiatric Study,"
by R. G. Druss, et al. JAMA 201:291-296, July 31, 1967.

"Time, Death, and the Ego-Chill," by A. Leveton J
EXIST 6:69-80, 1965.

"University of Kentucky Symposium: Sudden Cardiac Death.
Psychological Aspects of Sudden Cardiac Death," by F.
G. Surawicz HEART & LUNG 2:836-840, November/December,
1973.

PSYCHOTHERAPY FOR THE DYING
"Principles of Psychotherapeutic Terminal Care in Hospital Patients," by H. Freyberger DTSCH KRANKENPFLEGEZ
26:582-587, November, 1973.

"Psychological Death in Headshrinkers," by B. Schmidt,
et al. AM J PSYCHIAT 121:510-511, November, 1964.

"Psychotherapeutic Attitude of the Physician Toward Death," by G. Burloux THER UMSCH 27:75-77, February, 1970.

"Psychotherapy and the Patient with a Limited Life Span," by L. Leshan, et al. PSYCHIAT 24:318-323, November, 1961.

"Psychotherapy for the Dying," by H. Rosenthal AM J PSY-CHOTHERAP 2,3:626-633, July, 1957.

"Psychotherapy for the Dying Patient," by E. K. Ross CUR PSYCHIAT THER 10:110-117, 1970.

"Psychotherapy of the Dying Patient," by W. A. Cramond BRIT MED J 3:389-393, August 15, 1970.

"Therapy of the Terminally Ill Patient," by T Kostrubala ILL MED J 124:545-547, December, 1963.

PSYCHOTHERAPY GROUPS
"Reactions of a Psychotherapy Group to Ambiguous Circumstances Surrounding the Death of a Group Member," by D. D. Kirtley, et al. J CONSULT CLIN PSYCHOL 33:195-199, April, 1969.

"The Role of Death Fears in the Etiology of Phobic Anxiety as revealed in Group Psychotherapy," by L. Loeser, et al. INT J GROUP PSYCHOTHERAP 10,13: 287-297, July, 1960.

PSYCHOTIC BEHAVIOR
"Recent Parent Death and Mental Illness," by J. Birtchnell BRIT J PSYCHIAT 116:289-297, March, 1970.

"Schizophrenia and the Inevitability of Death," by H. F. Searles PSYCHIAT Q 35:631-665, October, 1961.

"Simultaneous Death in Schizophrenic Twins," by I. C. Wilson, et al. ARCH GEN PSYCHIAT 11:377-384, 1964.

"Sleep Paralysis, Psychosis, and Death," by S. C. Liddon AM J PSYCHIAT 126:1027-1031, January, 1970.

"Study of Parental Loss in Neurotics and Sociopaths," by S. Greer ARCH GEN PSYCHIAT 11:177-180, August, 1964.

RELIGION: CANCER PATIENTS

"Creative Support of a Cancer Patient," by R. D. Erickson BULL AM PROT HOSP ASS 34:15-21, #2, 1970.

RELIGION: CATHOLIC

"Catholic at the Non-Catholic Deathbed," by M. Beach
CATH WORLD 178:185-191, December, 1953.

"A Catholic Priest's Approach to the Sick," by D. Mullan IRISH NURS NEWS 10-5, March-April, 1967.

"How Coronary Patients Respond to Last Rites," by N. H.
Cassem, et al. POSTGRAD MED 45:147-152, 1969.

"Last Offices -- a Reassessment," by C. H. Thomas NURS
MIRROR 132:30, April 9, 1971.

"The Priest's Care of the Terminally Sick," by P. Lais-
ter NURS MIRROR 139:63-65, October 10, 1974.

"Word: Priest's Courage and Calm in Face of Death," by
V. P. McCorry AMERICA 93:572-573, September 10, 1955.

RELIGION: CHAPLAIN

"Chaplain -- A member of the Hospital Team. Ministering
to the Dying and Bereaved, by Boyling NM 120:599+,
September 17, 1965.

"Chaplain and the Dying Patient," by J. R. Cavanagh
HOSP PROG 52:34-40, November, 1971.

"The Hospital Chaplain ," by D. Pett NURS TIMES 69:1678-
1682, December 13, 1973.

"The Hospital Chaplain, Research and Pastoral Care," by
R. L. Carrigan PASTOR PSYCH 17,165:39-48, June, 1966.

"Hospital Chaplaincy Care of the Bereaved at the Time
of a Patient's Death," by R. B. Reeves, Jr. J PASTORAL
CARE 26:116, June, 1972.

"The Problem of Suffering," by Pare NM 120:556+, September 3, 1965.

"The Role of the Chaplain in Patient Relationships," by
J. Knowles J PASTORAL CARE 7,2:Summer, 1953.

RELIGION: CHAPLAIN

"The Theology of Death," by Montague NM 120:573+, September 10, 1965.

"Visiting the Sick," by Barton NM 120:527+, August 27, 1965.

RELIGION: CHILD'S DEATH
"Easter Child: Dealing with an Infant's Death within the Context of Christian Faith," by L. M. Tetlow AMERICA 130:284-286, April 13, 1974.

RELIGION: CHRISTIANITY AND DEATH
"All Saints and Souls," AMERICA 98:123, November 2, 1957

"Care of the Dying.7. Religion and the Care of the Dying," by R. Lamerton NURS TIMES 69:88-89, January 18, 1973.

"Christian Affirmation of Life," by K. D. O'Rourke HOSP PROG 55:65-7, July, 1974.

"Death and Christian Life," by R. W. Gleason AMERICA 96:124-125, November 3, 1956.

"Dialogue of Death: Freudian and Christian Views," by S. A. Banks PASTOR PSYCH 14,135:41-49, June, 1963.

"Essay Review: On Death and Theology," by H. Anderson THEOL TODAY 31:62-64+, April, 1974.

"Every Creature of God Is Good," by J. Gallagher CATH WORLD 171:437-439, September, 1950.

"Faith," by P. B. McCleave MINN MED 50:1054, July, 1967.

"Life and Death Question; Meaning of the Death of Christ for Christians," by W. J. Burghardt AMERICA 128:366-367, April 21, 1973.

"Life, Death and the Body in the Theory of Being," by H. Jonas R METAPHYS 19:3-23, September, 1965.

"Living Until Death," by R. G. Carey HOSP PROG 55:82-87, February, 1974.

"Need for a Theology of Death," by F. Minton CHR CENT 87:352-355, March 25, 1970: Discussion. 87:767-768, June 17, 1970.

"The Other Dimension: Spiritiual Help," by Piepgras AM J NURS 68:2610+, December, 1968.

"Psychotheological Treatise on Death," by R. C. Proctor N CAR MED J 28:467-468, November, 1967.

"Religion and the Care of the Dying," NURS TIMES 69:88-89, January 18, 1973.

"Standing in Awe," by M. E. Marty CHR CENT 90:551, May 9, 1973.

"Thanatos and Cain," by L. Szondi AM IMAGO 21:52-63, Fall, 1964.

"Theological Reflections on Death," by W. Carr N CAR MED J 28:461-464, November, 1967.

"Toward a New Morality of Death," by W. R. Yates RELIG IN LIFE 43:79-91, Spring, 1974.

"Two Sermons," by R. C. Bruce PROSE #8:39-44, Spring, 1974.

"Virtue, Death and Christmas," SPEC 211:840, December 27, 1963.

"Warning the Dying of Their Danger, In: Questions and Answers," by L. L. McReavy CLERGY REV 44:295-297, May, 1959.

"Why Bother About Life Beyond Death?" by G. M. Schnurr CHR CENT 83:424-426, April 6, 1966: Reply. E. T. Dahlberg. 83:806, June 22, 1966.

RELIGION: CLERGY/PHYSICIAN RELATIONSHIP
"Clergy -- Physician Dialogues," MARYLAND MED J 18:77-84, July, 1969.

RELIGION: CLERGY/PHYSICIAN RELATIONSHIP

"The Minister and the Physician as Working Partners," by
W. B. Oglesby, et al. PASTOR PSYCH 10:37-42, September,
1959.

"Physician and Minister Caring for the Terminal Patient,"
by L. C. Ratliff J MISS STATE MED ASS 13:202-207, May,
1972.

RELIGION: FEAR OF DYING
"Christian Maturity Dealing with the Problem of Death,"
by N. Von Hoffman RELIG IN LIFE 27:76-84, Winter, 1957-
1958.

"Death Anxiety in Religiously Very Involved Persons," by
D. I. Templer PSYCHOL REP 31:361-362, October, 1972.

"Old People Fight Death Worry Through Religion," SCI N L
68:182, September 17, 1955.

"Relation Between Death Anxiety, Belief in Afterlife, and
Locus of Control," by A. L. Berman, et al J CONSULT
CLIN PSYCHOL 41:318, October, 1973.

"The Relationship Between Religious Behavior and Concern
About Death," by D. Martin, et al. J SOC PSYCHOL 65:
317-323, April, 1965.

"Religion and Fears About Death: A Critical Review of
Research," by D. Martin, et al. RELIG ED 59:174-176,
March, 1964.

"Religiosity, Generalized Anxiety, and Apprehension Concerning Death," by R. L. Williams, et al. J SOC PSYCHOL
75:111-117, JUne, 1968.

RELIGION: HINDUISM
"Death and Kinship in Hinduism: Structural and Function-
al Interpretations," by H. Orenstein AM ANTHROP 72:
1357-1377, December, 1970.

RELIGION: JUDAISM
"Counseling the Bereaved," by R. L. Katz CCAR
YRBK 63:465-469, 1953.

RELIGION: JUDAISM

"The Dying and Their Treatment in Jewish Law," by I.
Jacobovits HEB MED J 2:242-251, 104-112, 1961.

"When Children Face Bereavement," CONS JUD 18:35-58,
1964.

RELIGION: MINISTERING TO THE DYING
"Behavior of Grief Stricken to Aid Clergy in Ministering
to Bereaved," THE NEW YORK TIMES 39:7, November 7,
1956.

"Death and Ministry: Death and Response," by R. Perske
PASTOR PSYCH 15:25-35, 1964.

"Ministering in a Death-Oriented Culture," by C. Miller
CHR TODAY 16:10-12, November 19, 1971.

"Ministering to the Bereaved and Dying," by L. C.
Pretty NED MED J 44:243-249, May, 1959.

"Ministering to the Dying," by C. A. Nighswonger BULL/
AM PROT HOSP ASS 34:117-124, #2, 1970.

"Ministering to the Dying As a Learning Encounter," by
C. A. Nighswonger J PASTOR CARE 26:86-92, June, 1972.

"Pastoral Care of the Dying and the Bereaved," by J.
Oakes DIST NURS 11:256-258, March, 1969.

"Pastoral Care of the Dying and the Bereaved," by J.
Oakes NURS J IND 60:371+, October, 1969.

"The Role of the Clergy in the Care of Seriously Ill
Patients,' by J. D. Shanahan ANN NY ACAD SCI 164:749-
758, December 19, 1969.

RELIGION: MOSLEM
"Muhammad's Thoughts on Death: A Thematic Study of the
Qur'anic Data," by T. O'Shaughnessy BRILL 83-86, 1969.

RELIGION: NURSING AND
"The Christian Nurse: A Nurse's Special Problems. 2.
Caring for the Dying," by H. Booth NURS TIMES 60:1615,
December 4, 1964.

RELIGION: NURSING AND

"Faith and Nursing," by Brown NURS TIMES 61:1428,
October 15, 1965.

RELIGION: PROBLEMS OF
"Hindrances to the Pastoral Care of the Dying," by J. W.
Steen PASTOR PSYCH 9,82:27-32, March, 1958.

RELIGION: PROTESTANT
"Dignity and Integrity in Dying (Insights from Early 19th
Century Protestantism," by R. V. Wells J PASTOR CARE
26:99-107, June, 1972.

SOCIAL WORK: CANCER
"Role of the Social Worker in a Children's Cancer Clinic,"
by A. Pieroni PEDIAT 40,3:534-536, September, 1967.

"Social Caseworkwith Cancer Patients," by R. D. Abrams
SOC CASE 32:425-433, 1951.

SOCIAL WORK: COUNSELING
"A Case Study of Social Crisis," by Brands NURS TIMES 64:
1167+, August 30, 1968.

"Casework with the Terminally Ill," by L. M. Weisberg
SOC CASE 55:337-342, June, 1974.

"Counseling of the Dying, Assistance During the Last
Illness," by J. J. Michels NED TIJDSCHR GENEESKD 117:
1944-1949, December 22, 1973.

"Existential Counseling for the Dying," by L. O. Bascue,
et al. J REHAB 38:18-19, March-April, 1972.

"Explore How Health Care Worker Can Ease Emotional Ills
of Dying," OR REPORTER 9:3+, June, 1974.

"In the Hour of Their Going Forth," by H. MacLaurin SOC
CASEWORK 40,3:136-140, March, 1959.

"An Interaction Study Involving a Patient with a Guarded
Prognosis," by L. McVay AM J NURS 66:1071-1073, May,
1966.

SOCIAL WORK: COUNSELING

"Problems of Impending Death. The Role of the Social
Worker," by R. Cowin PHYS THERAP 48:743-748, July,
1968.

"Role of the Local Authority Social Worker -- Catalyst
for Help in the Community," by P. Knight MIDWIFE
HEALTH VISIT 9:51-54, February, 1973.

"Social Casework and the Dying Person," by E. G. Gold-
stein SOC CASEWORK 54:601-608, December, 1973.

"Social Work and the Mourning Parent: The Case of the
Ill Child," by A. T. McCollum, et al. SOC WORK 17:
25-36, January, 1972.

"The Social Worker's Role," by M. P. Daniel BRIT MED J
1:36-38, January 6, 1973.

"Youville Hospital (Cambridge, Mass.) Program for Counseling the Dying," THE NEW YORK TIMES 44:1, January 21,
1973.

SOCIAL WORK: GENERAL
"Awareness Contexts and Social Interaction," by B. G.
Glaser, et al. AM SOC REV 29:669-679, 1964.

"Cultural Values and Attitudes Toward Death," by A.
Howard, et al. J EXIST 6:161-174, Winter, 1965-1966.

"Death and Dying: Towards a Sociological Understanding,"
by J. M. Najman HOSP HEALTH CARE ADMIN 3:7-9, May,
1973.

"Death and Interpersonal Failure," by D. F. Morgenson
CAN MENT HEALTH 21:10-12, May-August, 1973.

"Death and Social Structure," by R. Blauner PSYCHIAT 29:
378-394, November, 1966.

"Death and Social Values," by R. L. Fulton, et al. IND
J SOC RES 3:#2, 7-14, 1962.

"Death As a Social Phenomenon, Sociological Perspective
on Quality of Dying Patient's Care," by P. C. Thauber-
ger SOC SCI MED 8:437-448, August, 1974.

"Death in American Society -- A Brief Working Paper," by
T. Parsons AM BEHAV SCI 6:61-65, May, 1963.

"Fatal Illness: A Survey of Social Service Needs," by R.
R. Koenig SOC WORK 13:85-90, October, 1968.

"Illness of Social Work When Parents Are Faced with the
Fatal Illness of a Child," by P. A. Lang, et al. SOC
CASEWORK 49:161-166, March, 1968.

"The National Social Welfare Board and Death -- A Neglected Chance," by C. Blomquist LAKARTIDNINGEN 70:2566-
2567, July 11, 1973.

"The Psychodynamic Significance of Belief Regarding the
Cause of Serious Illness," by M. Bard, et al. PSYCHO-
ANAL REV 43:146-162, 1956.

"Psychosocial Aspects of Disease," by A. J. Lipowski ANN
INT MED 71:(6), 1197-1206, 1969.

"Social Distance and Dying," by R. A. Kalish COMMUN MENT
HEALTH J 2:152-155, 1966.

"Social Ecology of Dying: Observations of Wards for the
Terminally Ill," by D. K. Reynolds, et al. HOSP COMMUN
PSYCHIAT 25:147-152, March, 1974.

"The Social Loss of Dying Patients," by B. Glaser, et al.
AJN 64:119+, June, 1964.

"Social Problems Involving the Medical Care Team. 'Care
of the Dying,'" by K. P. Zabel KANSAS NURS J, 46:9,
November, 1971.

"Social Significance of the Danger List," by A. D. Weisman, et al. JAMA 215:1963-1966, March 22, 1971.

"Socioeconomic Differentials in Mortality by Cause of
Death," by M. H. Nagl, et al. HEALTH SERVS REPS 88:449-
456, May, 1973.

"Sociology of Death: A Neglected Area of Research," by
W. A. Faunce, et al. SOC FORCES 36:205-209, March, 1958.

SOCIAL WORK: GENERAL

"Some Correlates of Thoughts and Feelings Concerning
Death," by I. M. Greenberg, et al. NY HILL HOSP J
11,2/3:120-126, April-July, 1962.

"Working-Class Systems of Mutual Assistance in Case of
Childbirth, Illness, and Death," by H. A. Halbertsma
SOC SCI MED 3:321-330, January, 1970.

SOCIAL WORK: HOSPITAL MANAGEMENT AND
"How Social Work Can Influence Hospital Management of
Fatal Illness," by Z. P. Foster SOC WORK 30-35,
October, 1965.

THANATOLOGY
ALSO SEE EDUCATION
"Foundation of Thanatology," by A. Kutscher MENT HYG 53:
338-339, July, 1969.

"Foundation of Thanatology: Rationale and Functions," by
B. B. Schoenberg, et al. W MED J 16:20+, January-February, 1969.

"Interest in Thanatology," THE NEW YORK TIMES 105:4, November 10, 1974.

"New Medical Subspecialty, Thanatology, Is Studying the
Concerns of the Dying Patient and the Bereaved," MED
WORLD NEWS 12:30-36, May 21, 1971.

"New York City Symposium on Aid to Dying," THE NEW YORK
TIMES 23:1, December 30, 1972.

"Newly Formed Foundation of Thanatology Focuses on Death,"
AJN 69:1291-1292, June, 1969.

"Thanatology: A Study of 100 Deaths," by F. E. Lucente
TRANS AM ACAD OPTHALMOL OTOLARYNGOL 76:334-339, March-
April, 1972.

"Thanatology 1: College Courses," TIME 101:36, January
8, 1973.

"Thanatology: The Study of Death and the Care of the Dying," by S. V. Gullo BEDSIDE NURSE 5:11-14, May, 1972.

THANATOLOGY

"Thanatology Resurrected," by A. W. Cavins J IND MED ASS 61:1159, August, 1968.

"Thanatology (What to Tell a Child?)," TIME 67, March 14, 1969.

"Thanatopsis: Life's Last Stand," by S. Halpern AM IMAGO 21:23-36, Fall, 1964.

"Thanatopsis Revisited," by D. E. Gray J KANS MED SOC 73: 305, June, 1972.

"Thanatos," by J. R. Carballo CIBA SYMPOS 12:79-86, 1964.

TRANSPLANTS
"Theological Implications of Organ Transplants," by M. J. Hammond AORN J 9:53-56, March, 1969.

YOUNG ADULTS
"Twenty-Two Years Old and Dying of Leukemia," by N. Oraftik NURS FORUM 11:205-213, No. 2, 1972.

AUTHOR INDEX

Aasterud, M. 127
Abadi, M. 159
Abraham, C. 25
Abraham, H. S. 45
Abrahamsson, H. 1
Abram, H. S. 17, 109, 155.
Abrams, R. D. 44, 125, 171
Achte, K. A. 163
Adamek 136
Adelman, s. e. 49
Adler, C. S. 71
Adler, R. 77
Agate, J. 54
Agree, R. H. 35
Aguilera, D. C. 96
Agullera 88
Aitken-Swan, J. 45, 129
Alberts, M. E. 130
Alderson, M. R. 47, 51
Aldrich, C. K. 18, 152
Alexander, I. E. 13, 27, 69
Alexander, M. 20
Aldwinckle, R. F. 1
Allen, D. 1
Alson, M. 148
Alsop, S. 18, 132
Altman, L. L. 162
Alvarez, W. C. 51, 53, 61, 64, 94, 159
Ames, L. B. 82
Ammon, G. 163
Amyot, R. 91
Anders, R. I. 116

Anderson, E. 51
Anderson, H. 167
Anderson, W. F. 133, 138
Andersson, A. 103
Andre, H. B. 148
Andree, R. A. 102
Andrews, L. 90
Angrist, A. A. 160
Annis, J. W. 150
Ansohn, E. 110
Anthony, S. 1
Aries, P. 1
Aring, C. D. 23
Arling, C. 96
Arnold, J. D. 24
Arnstein, H. S. 1
Aronson, M. 158
Arthur, B. 66
Artiss, K. L. 126, 161
Assell, R. 157
Aunders, C. 50
Aurthur, R. A. 136
Autton, N. 36, 62
Auvinen, K. 57
Avorn, J. 113
Ayd, F. J. 64
Backers, A. 77
Bahnson, C. 45
Baker 34
Baker, J. M. 153
Bakke, J. L. 55, 64
Baltzell, W. H. 151
Banks, S. A. 167
Barber, T. X. 105
Barckley, V. 57, 131, 141
Barclay, D. 83
Bard, M. 173

176

Barnard, C. N. 143
Barnsteiner, J. H. 56, 64
Barrett, G. V. 160
Barrocas, A. 145
Barthel, J. 23, 147
Barton 167
Barton, D. 116, 120, 122, 123, 161
Bartz, W. R. 17, 28
Bascue, L. O. 171
Bates, R. C. 51
Batten, L. W. 142
Bax, H. R. 110, 151
Baxter, C. 65
Baxter, E. M. 100
Bayly, J. T. 1
Beach, M. 166
Beachy, W. N. 133
Beberman, A. 97
Becher, W. 125
Becker, A. H. 128
Becker, D. 82
Becker, E. 1
Becker, H. 164
Beigler, J. S. 16
Bell, D. W. 55
Bell, T. 1
Bellman, M. 72
Bellows, J. G. 51
Benavides, P. H. 59, 107
Bender, D. L. 1
Bennett, M. B. 52
Bennholdt-Thomsen, C 73, 77
Benoliel 68
Benoliel, J. G. 56, 59, 95, 130
Benson, G., Jr. 156
Berg, C. D. 70
Berg, D. W. 93, 122
Bergen, R. P. 55
Bergman, A. 61
Bergman, A. B. 80
Bergner, M. 60

Berman, A. L. 169
Berman, E. 2
Bernier, M. 106
Berry, R. 118
Bessho, C. 134
Bialowas, M. 27, 146
Bibring, G. L. 80
Bidrek, G. 112
Bigonesse, P. 73, 78
Biorck, G. 23, 27
Biran, S. 18, 106
Birren 55
Birtchnell, J. 18, 35, 67, 157, 160, 165
Blacher, R. S. 128
Blackmore, D. J. 148
Blank, J. 79
Blauner, R. 172
Blewett, L. J. 142
Blomquist, C. 173
Bluestone, H. 18, 132
Bock, H. E. 109
Boeker 46
Boelen, M. L. 53
Boger, J. 13
Boley, J. 103
Bonine, G. N. 82, 84
Booth, H. 170
Borkenau, F. 22
Borzoni, D. G. 47
Boshes, L. D. 131
Bouchard, J. 57
Bourguignon, A. 108
Bowen, A. 41
Bowen, O. R. 129
Bowne, E. 148
Bowlby 80
Bowlby, J. 2, 16, 35, 39, 66, 79
Boyers, R. 22
Boyling 166
Bozeman, M. 163
Brainard, F. 45
Branch, C. H. H. 154
Brands 171
Branson, H. K. 76, 136

Brauer 132
Brauer, P. 130
Brehant, J. 100, 128
Brennan, M. J. 44
Breed, J. E. 55
Breen, P. 104
Brickma-, H. R. 113
Bright, F. 79
Brill, N. 139
Brim, O. G. 2, 150
Brimigion, J. 120
Britton 133
Bro, M. H. 2
Brooke, B. N. 101
Brooks, R. P., Jr. 86
Brothers, J. 37
Brown 171
Brown, E., Jr. 15
Brown, J. E. 119
Brown, J. P. 58
Brown, N. K. 86
Browne, I. W. 17, 157
Bruce, R. C. 168
Bruhn, J. G. 17
Bryant, A. 135
Bucove, A. D. 156
Budge, E. A. W. 2
Buhrmann, M. V. 73, 80
Bulger, R. J. 108, 109
Bullock, A. 133
Burgert, E., Jr. 80
Burghardt, W. J. 167
Burloux, G. 165
Burnand, R. 92
Burnside 25, 39, 137
Burnside, I. M. 36
Burrell, R. J. 105
Burton, A. 156
Butler, R. N. 140
Buxbaum, R. E. 36, 109
Byers, M. L. 84
Caine, L. 2, 78, 81
Caldwell, J. R. 102
Callaway, E. 161
Calman, K. C. 43
Cameron, P. 26, 65, 98

Cameron, J. M. 131
Cancer Care Inc. 2
Canick, M. L. 130
Cantor, R. 46, 107
Caplan, G. 148
Capouya, E. 87
Cappon, D. 22, 23, 32, 89, 164
Caprio, F. S. 29, 115
Carballo, J. R. 174
Carey, R. G. 18, 54, 91, 167
Cargas, H. J. 88
Carlozzi, C. G. 2
Carmody, J. 97
Carnell, E. J. 19
Carpenter, J. 54
Carr, W. 168
Carrere, J. 155
Carrigan, R. L. 166
Carris, F. W. 120
Carson, J. 118
Cartwright, A. 2
Caruso, I. A. 106
Cassell, E. J. 118
Cassem, N. H. 17, 87, 166
Castels, M. M. 102
Caughill, R. E. 36
Cauton, T. 38
Cavanagh, J. R. 33, 166
Cavins, A. W. 174
Chaloner, L. 71
Chambon, J. 92, 159
Champagne, R. 86
Chanpigny, R. 86
Chandler, K. A. 102, 162
Chandra, R. K. 72
Charyk, W. 110
Chasin, B. 24
Chethik, M. 67
Childers, P. 70
Chodoff, P. 150, 154
Choron, J. 2
Christ, A. E. 26
Christenson, L. 111, 128
Chura, V. 60, 135, 142, 149

184

185

190

DATE DUE
